Practical Ways to Protect Yourself From Toxic People

Survival Guide for Recognizing Manipulation, Setting Boundaries, and Thriving in Every Relationship to Reclaim Yourself

George Munson

Copyright © 2025 by George Munson

All rights reserved

No portion of this book may be reproduced without written permission from the publisher or author except as permitted by U.S. copyright law.

This publication is designed to provide accurate and authoritative information regarding the subject matter covered. It is sold with the understanding that neither the author nor the publisher is engaged in rendering legal, investment, accounting, or other professional services.

While the publisher and author have used their best efforts in preparing this book, they make no representations or warranties with respect to the accuracy or completeness of the contents of this book and specifically disclaim any implied warranties of merchantability or fitness for a particular purpose. No warranty may be created or extended by sales representatives or written sales materials.

The advice and strategies contained herein may not be suitable for your situation. You should consult with a professional when appropriate. Neither the publisher nor the author shall be liable for any loss of profit or other commercial damages, including but not limited to special, incidental, consequential, personal, or other damages.

Neither the publisher nor the author claims responsibility for the persistence or accuracy of URLs for external or third-party Internet Websites referred to in this publication, and does not guarantee that any content on such Websites is, or will remain, accurate or appropriate.

Designations used by companies to distinguish their products are often claimed as trademarks. All brand names and product names used in this book and on its cover are trade names, service marks, trademarks and registered trademarks of their respective owners. The publishers and the book are not associated with any product or vendor mentioned in this book. None of the companies referenced within the book have endorsed the book.

First Edition 2025

Contents

Introduction   VII

1. Understanding the Toxic Landscape   1
   What Makes a Relationship Toxic?
   The Psychology Behind Manipulation and Control
   Red Flags: Recognize the Early Warning Signs in Everyday Interactions
   Demystifying the Toxic Labels of the Narcissist, Gaslighter, and Emotional Vampire
   How to Tell the Difference Between Toxic Patterns vs. Normal Conflict

2. The Language of Manipulation for Spotting Subtle Tactics   13
   Love Bombing and Hoovering are Recognizable and Manipulative Affection
   When Toxicity Spreads in Groups as Triangulation and Flying Monkeys
   When You're Accused of Their Behavior, that's Projection and Blame-Shifting

3. Mapping Your Personal Triggers and Vulnerabilities   25
   Why You Keep Attracting Toxic People

Identifying Your Own Emotional Triggers
　　　Scripts for Saying No to Break Free from People-Pleasing
　　　How Guilt and Obligation Are Used Against You
　　　Spotting and Challenging False Guilt
　　　Useful Scripts and Mental Reframes

4. Setting Boundaries Without Guilt　　　　　　　　　　36
　　　The Science of Boundaries and Why They Work
　　　How to Set Boundaries with a Toxic Parent Without Family Fallout
　　　Scripts for Enforcing Boundaries at Work (Even with a Difficult Boss)
　　　Know When to Set Limits and When to Walk Away In Navigating Friendships
　　　How to Handle Pushback or What to Do When Boundaries Trigger Backlash

5. Communication Blueprints for Difficult Conversations　　49
　　　Assertive Communication or How to Speak Up Without Fear
　　　De-Escalating Toxic Arguments With Language That Calms Instead of Fueling the Fire
　　　What to Say (And What Not to Say) When Responding to Gaslighting
　　　Use 'Gray Rock' and Minimal Contact to Master Neutral Responses
　　　Handling Public Manipulation When Toxic People Try to Shame You in Groups

6. Navigating Family, Parenting, and Shared Obligations　　62

Scripts and Safety Plans for Parallel Parenting with a Toxic Ex
   Protecting Your Children from Toxic Relatives
   Managing Sibling Dynamics When a Parent Is Toxic
   Caring for a Toxic Elder Can Require Balancing Duty and Self-Protection
   How to Explain Boundaries to Partners and "Non-Believers"

7. Protecting Yourself Professionally from Toxicity at Work   74
   Spotting the Toxic Boss Includes Behaviors You Can't Ignore
   Scripts for Handling Manipulative Coworkers in Meetings
   Protecting Your Reputation from Gossip and Smear Campaigns
   Documenting Toxic Behavior With Paper Trails and HR Strategies
   What to Do If You're Targeted After Speaking Up (Retaliation)

8. Healing, Recovery, and Rebuilding Self-Worth   89
   Unlearning Self-Blame and Shame
   Journaling Prompts for Reclaiming Self-Esteem
   Mindfulness and Grounding Practices for Emotional Recovery
   Find Your "Chosen Family" to Build a Resilient Support System
   Restoring Trust in Yourself and Others After Betrayal

9. Prevention and Pattern-Breaking for the Future   101
   Creating Your Personal Red Flag Checklist
   How to Vet for Toxic Traits Early When Dating and Building New Friendships
   Teaching Your Children Healthy Boundaries to Stop the Cycle

    Navigating Social Media and Digital Boundaries

    When to Seek Professional Help Through Therapy, Support Groups, and Legal Resources

10. Live Free and Thrive Beyond Toxic Relationships   113

    Designing a Life That Attracts Healthy Relationships

    Daily Boundary Rituals that Create Habits for Long-Term Emotional Safety

    Celebrating Progress to Honor Your Journey and Stay Empowered

Conclusion   124

References   128

Introduction

You're sitting across from someone you know, such as a partner, parent, friend, or boss. The conversation starts innocently, but soon it takes a turn. Your stomach tightens as their words and tones turn harsh.

Suddenly, you find yourself apologizing for something you never intended to do. Later, you ask yourself, "Was I to blame?" Or "Am I being too sensitive?" Recognizing these signs early is crucial for change, and this book is here to support you on that journey.

Often, it isn't very clear. It's draining. Sometimes it's hard to put your finger on what's wrong. You may feel guilty about feeling bad or question whether your emotions are real. Maybe you even worry that you're the problem. For example, a friend who constantly criticizes your choices or a boss who dismisses your efforts. I know these feelings because I hear them repeatedly from people who reach out for help. The shame, the self-doubt, and the loneliness can feel overwhelming.

After years of people recognizing and healing from toxic relationships, whether in families, workplaces, friendships, or romantic partnerships, I understand how challenging it can be to break free from old patterns. Often, it's difficult to identify what's happening or why you feel so stuck. My work has been fueled by listening to countless stories and by my own journey through complex relationships. This book aims to provide you with clear guidance and practical tools to find real answers and supportive solutions that genuinely work.

So, what do I mean by "toxic people"? In this book, a toxic person is not merely someone who has a bad day or is challenging to deal with; we all make mistakes. Toxicity refers to a repeated pattern of behavior that undermines your confidence, well-being, and sense of self. It might be the friend who constantly criticizes or competes with you, the partner who manipulates or controls, the family member who ignores your needs, or the boss who takes credit for your work, leaving you doubting your abilities. These are not just one-time slip-ups; they are ongoing cycles that can leave you feeling small, stuck, or powerless.

You might be wondering if your situation is "bad enough" to count. You can't just leave because of family ties, work contracts, financial limits, or cultural pressure. Or perhaps you're not even sure what's wrong, only that something is off, and you want things to change. You don't have to have all the answers, and you don't have to do this alone.

What makes this book different? I wanted to create a resource I wished I'd had years ago, one that doesn't just describe the problem but guides you through it. Inside, you'll find step-by-step strategies for spotting toxic patterns, like a friend who constantly criticizes or a boss who dismisses your efforts, real-life scripts for tough conversations, and simple explanations of why these dynamics happen. My goal is to empower you with practical tools and relatable stories so you can take concrete steps toward healthier relationships. You'll find guidance for complicated family dynamics, work challenges, and friendships that leave you questioning your worth. Most of all, you'll get support that honors your reality, not someone else's idea of what you "should" do.

This book provides readers with practical strategies to identify toxic behaviors, develop effective boundary-setting skills that enhance self-confidence, and implement tools designed to safeguard mental and emotional well-being. You will learn how to speak for yourself, let go of guilt, and feel confident in your own choices. I hope that you'll finish this book with a stronger sense of self, better relationships, and a path forward that feels right for you.

I know many fears come with this work. Maybe you're worried about upsetting people, or you've tried to change things before, and it didn't work. Perhaps you feel trapped by family or work obligations, or you fear what others will think. I want you to know if this book meets you where you are; there's no judgment here for staying, leaving, or simply struggling with boundaries. Life is complicated, and your experience is valid.

Here's how the book is set up. First, we'll look at what toxic behavior really is, how to spot it, and why it happens. Next, you'll learn how to set boundaries and communicate your needs, even when it feels impossible.

Then, we'll dig into specific situations, family, work, friendships, and romantic relationships, so you have practical steps for real-life challenges. Finally, we'll talk about healing, self-care, and building the support you need to thrive, even after long-term exposure to toxic people.

If you've ever wondered whether things can get better, the answer is yes. You have more power than you think. This book is your guide, your toolkit, and your source of encouragement as you step toward safer, healthier relationships. You don't have to stay stuck. Real change is possible, and you are worth it. Let's take these steps together.

Chapter One

Understanding the Toxic Landscape

I once overheard a woman in a coffee shop whispering to her friend about her partner: "I just never know if today will be a good day or if I'll get the 'silent treatment' for something I don't even remember doing." Her friend looked unsure how to respond, but that sense of tension and self-doubt is so common. Many people live on edge, constantly questioning if they're overreacting or just being sensitive. You might find yourself revisiting old arguments, trying to pinpoint where things went wrong, or blaming yourself for not keeping the peace. You're not alone. This chapter aims to clarify what truly makes a relationship toxic and help you identify the signs that are easily overlooked or minimized.

What Makes a Relationship Toxic?

A toxic relationship is defined by recurring negative patterns that leave you feeling drained, anxious, and not good enough. It's not just a single nasty fight or rough patch; everyone goes through those. The difference lies in the repetitive cycle of behaviors that slowly erodes your confidence and happiness. In a healthy relationship, you feel able to be yourself, express your needs, and trust that disagreements won't be used against you later. Respect, support, and mutual growth are expected. Even when mistakes occur, you can discuss them and move forward without fear of backlash or sabotage.

Contrast this with a toxic partnership. For example, a disagreement about weekend plans in a healthy relationship involves honest discussion and sometimes compromise. Still, both people feel heard and safe. In a toxic dynamic, even minor issues can escalate into days of cold shoulders or cutting remarks. Your partner may mock your opinions, make you feel foolish, or dig up past mistakes to shame you. The tension builds, and you start doubting the validity of your own needs.

This pattern isn't confined to romantic relationships. At work, a boss might alternate between praise and harsh criticism unpredictably, leaving you anxious and off-balance. Among friends or family, toxicity may appear as recurrent guilt trips or criticism meant to sound "honest." Whether at home, at work, or with friends, toxicity is marked by persistent disrespect or routine boundary violations, resulting in walking on eggshells far too often.

Toxicity is about sustained patterns, not one forgotten birthday or a single stressful week. If someone routinely ignores your boundaries, belittles your successes, or unpredictably shifts between kindness and cruelty, the ground starts feeling unstable. Often called "charm and harm," this cycle is confusing because moments of kindness give hope that things will change, even as the negative patterns persist.

The impact on your well-being is significant. Living with constant anxiety about someone's reactions or avoiding specific topics to keep the peace causes ongoing stress, slowly undermining your ability to trust yourself. You might second-guess your memory, stay nervous even in safe settings, or notice the toll on your work, friendships, and even your physical health, headaches, trouble sleeping, and more.

Doubts are common; maybe you wonder whether it's really 'that bad' or whether calling a relationship toxic is too harsh. These feelings especially arise when the toxicity builds gradually over time, affecting your mental health. Take Mia, who excused her friend's digs as harmless jokes, only to realize, years later, the chronic disrespect and diminished self-worth. If harm is subtle, self-questioning comes easily; toxic relationships often grow insidiously, slowly eroding your confidence and sense of stability.

Let's Take a Moment

Think about a relationship where you felt uneasy or anxious before seeing the person, or relieved when plans were canceled. Write down three specific behaviors or moments that made you feel small, confused, or drained. For example, did they dismiss your opinions or make you feel guilty? This exercise helps you recognize patterns without judgment and increases your awareness of red flags.

Recognizing toxicity involves noticing these ongoing patterns: consistent behaviors like belittling successes or boundary violations that gradually undermine your well-being and self-esteem. Highlighting these specific red flags helps readers more clearly identify the repetitive nature of toxic dynamics.

The Psychology Behind Manipulation and Control

Why do some people always need the upper hand in every interaction? It's not always about a grand plan to hurt others. Often, it's a tangled knot of insecurity, fear, and an urge to avoid feeling powerless. People who act in manipulative ways might crave control because, deep down, they are terrified of rejection or vulnerability. Sometimes, they grow up in chaotic homes, learning that controlling others is the only way to feel safe. Other times, it's a learned habit: if you always get your way by twisting the truth or guilt-tripping someone, you keep doing it. Recognizing these underlying motives helps you understand manipulation tactics used to maintain control.

The tactics toxic people use to hold onto that power range from slick to downright sneaky. Gaslighting is a favorite; this happens when someone distorts reality, denying things you remember clearly or insisting you're too sensitive. You might say, 'That hurt my feelings,' and they respond with, 'You're imagining things; I never said that.' After enough rounds of this, you begin questioning your own memory, which erodes your self-trust. Then there's love-bombing, an overwhelming flood of affection, attention, or gifts early in a relationship or after a fight. It feels intoxicating at first; suddenly, you're the center of their world. But soon it turns conditional. If you step out of line or assert yourself, the warmth disappears. Stonewalling, or giving the 'silent treatment', is another classic move used to punish or regain control without saying a word. The message is clear: you don't get my attention until you behave the way I want, which chips away at your confidence and sense of safety.

Manipulation isn't always loud or dramatic. It can creep in so quietly that you hardly notice until you're deep in self-doubt. Imagine this: every time you raise a concern, your partner sighs and plays the wounded one, so you end up comforting them instead of getting your needs met. Over time, you tell yourself it's easier not to speak up at all. Eventually, your feelings seem less important than keeping the peace. This is how self-blame grows, slowly but relentlessly. Each cycle chips away at your confidence, making you wonder if you're too needy or not strong enough.

What makes these tactics so powerful is their subtlety. Rarely does manipulation show up as a neon sign saying, "You're being controlled!" Instead, it comes disguised as concern ("I just want what's best for you"), fake apologies ("I'm sorry you feel that way"), or even compliments with strings attached ("You're amazing when you listen to me"). These patterns mess with your mind, leaving you confused and questioning your instincts. Toxic people thrive on this confusion because it keeps you off-balance and easier to control.

It's common to feel guilty for not catching on sooner or for letting things go as far as they have. But manipulation is designed to slip under your radar. It builds gradually, often disguised as love, humor, or helpfulness. You might tell yourself stories to explain away the weirdness: "They've had a stressful day," "Maybe I did overreact," "It's probably just me." These thoughts are everyday, and they don't mean you're weak or naive.

Manipulators are skilled at turning situations so that you doubt your own judgment.

Consider the slow erosion of self-trust that results from repeated manipulation. Picture someone who starts out feeling confident and outspoken but gradually becomes hesitant and anxious about every little thing, what to say, how to say it, whether they'll set off another round of silent treatment or blame. Their world shrinks as they second-guess every move. This isn't a failure on their part; it's the intended effect of persistent mind games.

Understanding these motivations and tactics strips away some of their power over you. Recognizing how fear of vulnerability or loss of control can drive someone to manipulate helps put their behavior in perspective; it's about them, not a flaw in you. If any of this sounds uncomfortably familiar, remember that noticing these patterns is the first step toward reclaiming your sense of self and finding your voice again.

Red Flags: Recognize the Early Warning Signs in Everyday Interactions

Red flags rarely announce themselves. More often, they appear subtly, small moments that leave you second-guessing. Someone says, "Just this once, can't you...?" pushing you to do something that feels wrong. Or a friend gives a compliment with a sting, I wish I could pull off your style, but I'd look sloppy", leaving you unsure if it was praise or criticism. These kinds of red flags often seem almost normal, but over time, they add up.

Let's say you're at work. Your boss "jokes" about your mistake in front of the team; you laugh along, but later feel embarrassed and resentful. If this happens more than once, it's a sign that your boundaries aren't being respected. Or imagine a family member who only calls when they need something. If you say you're busy, they remind you of all they've done for you, leaving you apologizing for no reason.

Red flags may manifest themselves differently across different types of relationships. In romantic contexts, this could include a partner who consistently monitors your whereabouts, implies that your friends are unsupportive, or creates barriers to spending time with loved ones. Within the workplace, it may be evident in colleagues who claim ownership of your ideas or interrupt you during meetings while maintaining a cordial relationship with management. Among friends, red flags might manifest as exclusion from group activities or teasing that is perceived as derisive rather than playful.

Here's a Quick Checklist for Red Flags

- Repeatedly pushing your boundaries ("Just this once...", "Don't be so uptight!")

- Criticism disguised as compliments ("I'd never have the guts to wear that!")

- Isolating you from others (discouraging your time with friends/family)

- Words and actions that don't match ("I support you," but then undermining your choices)

- Playing the victim when confronted ("I can't believe you'd accuse me after all I do for you.")

- Shifting blame onto you ("If you weren't so sensitive, we wouldn't fight.")

- Violating your privacy (snooping, reading your messages)

- Making you feel guilty for setting boundaries ("I guess I'll just be alone, then.")

Most warning signs are not dramatic. Sometimes it's simply feeling uneasy when someone crosses a line and laughs it off. Other times, it's realizing you're seeing loved ones less because it's too stressful to keep explaining yourself. Trust these instincts. Suppose you constantly second-guess your words, avoid specific topics, or mentally rehearse conversations. In that case, you might be dealing with chronic disrespect. In healthy relationships, you don't need to overthink each interaction; you feel safe being honest, even during disagreements.

Let's look at some scenarios. In families, a sibling who always asks for favors and calls you selfish if you say no may be exploiting your goodwill. At work, a boss who assigns last-minute projects but criticizes you in public and praises you in private is keeping you off-balance. In dating, a partner who alternates between over-the-top affection and coldness can leave you anxious and eager to regain their approval.

If any of these examples feel familiar, take note. It can help to document these incidents by jotting down what was said, how you felt, and whether it's happened before. Over time, patterns will become clearer, even if each event seems minor on its own. Recording details helps clarify confusion and reveal the reality.

Trust your intuition. Even if you can't immediately label what's wrong, pay attention to repeated discomfort or disrespect. Red flags rarely occur just once; they repeat in different forms. You deserve relationships where your needs are respected, and you can speak honestly without fear or guilt. Noticing patterns and writing them down helps you trust your instincts and choose your next steps with confidence.

Demystifying the Toxic Labels of the Narcissist, Gaslighter, and Emotional Vampire

It's hard to scroll through social media or to overhear a conversation these days without someone tossing out words like "narcissist" or "gaslighter." These terms have become part of everyday language, but they're often misused or misunderstood. When you hear "narcissist," think of someone who consistently puts their own needs and desires ahead of everyone else's, no matter what the cost. It's not just about liking their reflection or taking a lot of selfies; it's about a pattern of self-centered, manipulative actions that leave others feeling used or invisible. Maybe you've known someone who always turns conversations back to themselves, ignores your boundaries, and expects special treatment while refusing to do the same for you. That's the heart of narcissistic behavior: an ongoing sense of entitlement and a lack of genuine empathy for other people.

A gaslighter, on the other hand, specializes in making you doubt your own reality. This isn't just a one-off white lie; it's a routine strategy. Imagine mentioning something that happened last week, maybe a difficult conversation or a promise that was broken, and the other person flat-out denies it ever took place. They might say, "That never happened," or, "You must be confused." Over time, these small denials pile up, making you second-guess your memory and even your sanity. Gaslighting works because it's subtle and persistent. You start feeling unsure about things you once knew for sure, and the person gaslighting you uses that confusion to keep control.

Then there are the emotional vampires, a label that captures people who leave you feeling drained after every interaction. They seem to suck all the energy out of the room. These folks always find a way to make every issue about themselves. If you share good news, they quickly redirect the spotlight to their own stories or problems. If you're in pain, they either dismiss it or use it as a jumping-off point to talk about their own struggles. You might leave a lunch date with them feeling like you've run a marathon without ever getting a chance to share your own thoughts or feelings.

It's tempting to stick these labels on anyone who annoys us or causes drama, but caution is necessary. Careless labeling can do real damage to relationships that might otherwise be repaired or improved. I remember seeing two friends fall out over one calling the other a narcissist during an argument about forgotten plans. The label stuck, even though the behavior was more about thoughtlessness than an actual pattern of manipulation. Once these terms are out there, it's hard to take them back, and it can shut down honest communication.

At the same time, having names for these patterns is incredibly powerful when used thoughtfully. Labels like narcissist, gaslighter, and emotional vampire help put words to confusing experiences. They give you vocabulary for what's happening, something that feels slippery and hard to explain otherwise. When you can say, "My boss keeps denying things she said last week," or "My partner always makes everything about himself," it becomes easier to see what's really happening and start looking for solutions instead of endlessly blaming yourself.

The point is not to diagnose others or paint them as villains, but to give yourself clarity and language for what you're living through. Sometimes just naming these patterns lifts some of the fog; suddenly, you realize it's not just you being too sensitive or dramatic. It's a set of well-known behaviors with predictable effects on how you feel and function. Recognizing these patterns lets you take your next steps, whether that means setting firmer boundaries, seeking outside support, or simply knowing you're not alone in your experience.

Misuse of these terms can muddy the waters and cause unnecessary hurt. Still, when applied thoughtfully and responsibly, they shine a light on what's really going on behind the scenes in complex relationships. That light helps you move from confusion to understanding, and from there, toward protecting yourself in new ways.

How to Tell the Difference Between Toxic Patterns vs. Normal Conflict

Everyone argues sometimes, even in the healthiest relationships; disagreements happen. What distinguishes typical conflict from a toxic pattern is what follows and how these moments accumulate. Healthy conflict lets both people express their feelings, even when emotions run high. There's room for apologies, listening, and real resolution. While you might feel upset during the argument, you also sense respect and that your feelings matter. For example, you might disagree with a friend about plans, but you still trust they want to understand you, not hurt or punish you. After tempers cool, someone reaches out to clear the air and move the relationship forward.

In toxic patterns, arguments become power struggles or emotional weapons. Think of a recurring fight where the other person refuses to talk, slams doors, or glares across the room for days. Instead of resolving an issue, the disagreement becomes a punishment or means of control. No apology follows, just blame-shifting or silent resentment. You may even be expected to pretend nothing happened, as if your pain doesn't count. The cycle repeats, leaving you feeling more isolated each time.

To clarify confusing moments, ask yourself: Does this disagreement lead to better understanding, or does it leave me anxious and uncertain? Healthy conflict seeks resolution; toxic patterns escalate tension and never resolve the underlying problem.

Here are Some Questions to Decide if This is a Normal Conflict or a Toxic Pattern

- Did both people have a chance to speak?

    - Yes: Healthy

    - No: Potential toxicity

- Was there any apology or attempt at repair?

    - Yes: Healthy

    - No: Red flag

- Does the issue keep resurfacing in the same way?

    - No: Healthy

- Yes: Ongoing pattern, watch closely
- Do you feel safe expressing your feelings?
  - Yes: Healthy
  - No: Take note, this may point to deeper issues
- Does the aftermath involve punishment (silent treatment, guilt trips)?
  - No: Healthy
  - Yes: This is toxic territory

Checking more boxes on the toxic side means you should take your gut feelings seriously.

Another clue is the "drama triangle," where people switch between three roles: victim ("Why does this always happen to me?"), persecutor ("This is your fault!"), and rescuer ("Let me fix this for everyone!"). In toxic conflict, these roles continuously shift. You might defend yourself at first, then apologize for things you didn't do, or find yourself comforting someone who just hurt you. The tension becomes an emotional tug-of-war; nobody wins for long. Healthy relationships don't trap people in these roles; instead, each person owns their feelings without shifting blame or demanding rescue.

Toxic dynamics can be confusing because they include occasional kindness. You might think, "Maybe things aren't so bad; they were sweet to me yesterday." That hope, fed by brief kindness, makes the cycle harder to recognize. But suppose kindness is always overshadowed by more chaos or withdrawal. In that case, it's not a real repair; it's just another round in the cycle.

You may feel frustrated with yourself for missing these patterns or rationalizing them. It's normal to wonder if you're being too sensitive or expecting too much. Toxic conflict clouds judgment, making it difficult to separate love from obligation or fear from loyalty. The good news? Each time you identify these cycles, you gain clarity and confidence.

As you notice these differences and trust your instincts, it gets easier to know which relationships are worth investing in and which are draining you. Repair, respect, and safety are the cornerstones of any worthwhile connection. If those are missing and conflict always feels like a trap, it might be time to reconsider your next steps.

You don't have to accept cycles that leave you confused or minimized. Healthy disagreements allow space for both voices and real progress. Seeing these patterns for what they are, without self-blame, is the first step. That awareness makes room for new choices and stronger boundaries in the future.

Chapter Two

The Language of Manipulation for Spotting Subtle Tactics

Understanding how gaslighting works is essential for recognizing when your reality is being twisted so that you can identify subtle manipulation tactics early. Imagine bringing up a conversation from last week about a stinging comment or a split-chore discussion. The other person insists, "That never happened. You must be imagining things." You clearly remember, yet their certainty makes you doubt yourself. This is gaslighting, one of the stealthiest manipulation tactics, like when someone dismisses your feelings about an incident to make you question your memory.

Gaslighting is more than lying or forgetting. It's an intentional pattern where someone consistently distorts the truth to make you question your memory, senses, or judgment. Honest disagreement sounds like, "I remember it differently," letting both perspectives coexist. Gaslighting, however, shuts you down: "You must be confused; that never happened," erasing your reality and planting self-doubt.

Gaslighting typically starts small. Minor denials, like brushing off a broken promise, become routine. Maybe you say, "Didn't you promise to pick up the kids?" and hear, "Nope, I never said that," even though you'd just discussed it. The denials intensify. Some gaslighters hide or move things (like your keys or wallet), then play innocent and claim, "You're always losing things," or insist you never owned the item. Another trick is questioning your judgment or sanity: "Are you sure you're okay? You seem forgetful lately." These aren't random but calculated, aiming to keep you off balance and reliant on their narrative.

Eventually, denial escalates to full-blown rewriting of events. The gaslighter might recast a heated argument as a friendly chat or claim it never happened. If you defend your memory, they double down: "You always make things bigger than they are," or, "You're too sensitive." This isn't a matter of faulty memory on both sides; it's one person trying to invalidate the other's experience.

The impact is subtle yet powerful. Initially, you might dismiss incidents as misunderstandings. But as they accumulate, you start doubting your memory, feelings, even your sanity. At first, you're confident in what happened; soon, you're apologizing to end arguments. Anxiety builds. You might suppress your thoughts or avoid sensitive topics to prevent more denial. Over time, your confidence decays. You wonder whether you're losing your mind or whether anyone would see things the way you do.

Consider Jenna, whose partner repeatedly denies making agreements with her, causing her to doubt herself and feel increasingly isolated. When she brings up broken promises, he brushes them off, "You must have misunderstood me." Jenna resorts to writing notes after conversations to keep herself grounded when her memories are again dismissed. Over time, her self-trust wanes, and she hesitates to raise important issues.

Gaslighting feeds on secrecy and confusion. One key defense: keep your own reality log to document interactions and stay grounded

Here's a Personal Gaslighting Checklist

Recognize manipulation tactics and protect your mental health.

- When someone denies an event, ask yourself: Did I experience this directly?

- Keep a running log (on paper or your phone) of questionable interactions.

- If you feel anxious or confused after a specific conversation, write down precisely what was said.

- Look for patterns. Do these incidents happen mostly with one person?

- Use grounding statements like, "My experience is valid, even if someone else denies it."

- Check in with a trusted friend about your recollection for an outside perspective.

If you suspect gaslighting, remember that honest people may forget details or disagree, but they don't try to erase your reality or undermine your sanity. Consistent documentation offers both clarity and self-protection. Over time, these steps help regain trust in your perceptions and rebuild solid ground under your feet.

Love Bombing and Hoovering are Recognizable and Manipulative Affection

Something is thrilling when someone showers you with attention, praise, or affection from the start. Maybe they claim you're the most amazing person they've ever met, or they give you thoughtful gifts, spontaneous trips, or grand gestures before you're even comfortable. This excitement can sweep you off your feet, making you feel truly seen and valued, but that's the trap of love bombing, the deliberate use of overwhelming affection to push the relationship forward unnaturally fast. Hence, you bond quickly and overlook red flags. If someone is excessively eager or makes you feel like royalty overnight, pause and ask: Is this genuine, or am I being manipulated?

Often, love bombing is followed by hoovering. After the adoration fades, the same person may suddenly become cold or distant. They might react harshly when you set boundaries or withdraw all attention, leaving you confused and craving the warmth you've lost. Just as you begin to move on or establish distance, they return, maybe with dramatic apologies, gifts, or promises that this time is different. You might get a nostalgic, regretful message, or a surprise delivery after weeks of silence. This cycle of affection and withdrawal is meant to keep you off balance and longing for their approval.

You can also spot this pattern in subtler ways. Perhaps, after an argument in which you finally spoke up, they send flowers or long texts professing their love. Or every time you assert a boundary, by asking for space, saying no, or requesting respect, they counter with a dramatic gesture or show of vulnerability. These aren't just attempts to "try hard"; they're strategies to regain control and keep you emotionally hooked. The affection always comes with invisible strings: "If you really loved me, you'd let this go," or "I only get upset because I care." You may feel guilty for wanting space or worry that saying no will "ruin everything."

A major red flag is how quickly the mood shifts from affection to distance or even punishment, and then back again. If someone adores you one day but is cold or punishing the next, only to return with more gifts or praise, it's time to question whether their affection is a tool for control. Genuinely caring people respect your space and don't use warmth as leverage. If requests always follow compliments, or if kindness only appears after conflict, take note.

Suppose you notice love bombing or hoovering, slow things down and give yourself space to think clearly. Instead of being swept away by attention or guilted by sudden apologies, try using a script: "I appreciate your kindness, but I need some time to process my feelings," or "Thank you for reaching out, but I'm not ready to reconnect yet." These responses protect your boundaries without escalating drama or giving up your power. If you do reconnect later, make sure it's on your terms, not because you were pressured into it by gifts, apologies, or declarations of love.

Setting clear limits is hard when emotions run high. You might need to repeat yourself: "I'm taking time to figure out what I want," or "I need actions, not words, to believe things will change." Watch for strings; genuine affection isn't conditional or used to mask repeated hurtful behavior. Document your own feelings and responses. Writing down what happens after each round of attention or withdrawal helps you trust your instincts and recognize patterns.

Love bombing and hoovering are so powerful because they exploit our natural desire for closeness and validation. It's normal to want affection and appreciation, but what matters is whether it's given freely or dangled like bait. You deserve relationships where warmth and care are consistent, not used as weapons to keep you off balance. When in doubt, take a breath and remember that real love doesn't require you to surrender your boundaries or self-respect to keep someone happy.

When Toxicity Spreads in Groups as Triangulation and Flying Monkeys

Manipulation isn't always one-on-one; often, toxic people create drama by involving others. Triangulation is a common tactic: instead of addressing issues directly, a poisonous person brings in a third party, leaving you caught in the middle. Suddenly, people are picking sides, trust erodes, and the manipulator sits back, enjoying the tension. They might say to a coworker, "Did you hear what she said about you?" or tell your sibling, "Mom is really disappointed in your choices." Quickly, groups turn against each other, all orchestrated by the original instigator.

Flying monkeys become involved when a toxic individual recruits others, intentionally or not, to push their agenda. This could be a partner telling friends only part of a story so they'll pressure you to "be nicer," or a boss who subtly encourages coworkers to report on each other. In families, it shows up when messages are relayed through siblings rather than spoken directly: "Tell your brother he needs to call me." In friend groups, a single manipulative whisper that you're "always negative" can fracture the entire group, leaving you confused and excluded.

This indirect communication replaces honesty with gossip and division. A toxic boss might complain about one employee to another, breeding mistrust and competition. Friends and colleagues start taking sides, often without knowing the whole story. Rumors and misunderstandings grow, fueling drama while the instigator remains on the sidelines. Triangulation muddies communication, making it difficult to resolve problems head-on and leaving you unsure of whom to trust or what's true.

The emotional impact builds quietly. You become tense around group events or avoid certain people due to a hostile atmosphere. Minor miscommunications blow up into major rifts, and relationships crumble over issues that could have been resolved in a direct conversation. Work teams stop collaborating, friendships dissolve, and families become distant. Tight-knit friend groups have broken apart because one person manipulated everyone else into "choosing sides," turning a minor argument into an irreparable divide.

You don't have to accept this chaos. The first step to escaping the triangle is to avoid passing along messages or gossip. If someone tries to involve you with, "Did you hear what so-and-so said about you?" respond with, "If you have an issue with them, you should talk to them directly." If asked to weigh in on someone else's conflict, establish a boundary: "I'd rather not get involved. If they want to talk to me, they can." These responses prevent being used as a pawn and show that you won't tolerate manipulation.

Direct communication is key. If someone brings you a complaint from another, don't react defensively or join in. Say, "I'd be happy to discuss this with them directly if there's a problem." When others urge you to take sides, respond, "I don't want to take sides. I hope you two can work it out." These approaches clear up communication and isolate the manipulator's tactics, reducing their effectiveness.

It's hard not to get drawn into drama, especially when group emotions run high. But redirecting conversations to direct communication and refusing to engage in others' conflicts chips away at group manipulation. Honesty and transparency prevent toxic people from using you or the group as instruments for their own ends. Protecting yourself in these situations doesn't just maintain your peace; it helps restore trust in your circles. When people see you resisting manipulation, they may follow your example, encouraging healthier group dynamics.

Let's Take an Inventory for Group Manipulation

Think about recent times you felt pressured to take sides or relay messages. Who was involved? What was the real issue? Was the communication direct, or through a third party? For each event, ask, "Did I feel connected afterwards, or did I feel isolated?" Use these reflections to spot patterns and practice stepping out of triangles before they become traps.

Scripts for Spotting Covert Control, such as Guilt-Tripping and Emotional Blackmail

There's a unique pain in feeling responsible for someone else's happiness, especially when they offload it onto you. Guilt-tripping and emotional blackmail manipulate your empathy, making you feel selfish or heartless if you don't comply. Phrases like "After all I've done for you, this is how you treat me?" or "If you cared, you'd do this for me" aren't valid requests; they're traps. Suddenly, you're anxious and scrambling to please, even when it feels unfair. Toxic people use guilt as a way to control, tugging at you whenever you assert yourself.

Healthy requests respect your choice and right to say no: "Would you help me move this weekend?" is straightforward. In contrast, requests that come with strings or threats, "If you don't help, I guess I'll just manage alone. Don't be surprised if I stop calling", thus signaling emotional blackmail. The silent treatment after you set a boundary isn't about disappointment; it's punitive, meant to pull you back in line. The message is clear: your needs are secondary, and independence is met with coldness or drama.

The language of emotional blackmail is often recognizable: "You're selfish if you won't help me," "I guess I can't count on you after all," or "If you don't do this, I'll never speak to you again." These aren't innocent comments; they're designed to press your buttons and compel you to comply. Sometimes it's even subtler: a dramatic sigh, a wounded look, or exiting the room after you set a limit. The constant is the expectation that their pain or disappointment is your responsibility to fix.

Spotting these red flags in the moment takes practice. Try pausing and imagining it happening to a friend. Does it seem fair? Would you expect a friend to give in to keep things smooth? Manipulation is often easier to recognize at a distance. Notice patterns: Does this person contact you only when they need something? Do they react with anger or withdrawal when you say no? Does helping them leave you feeling drained or resentful?

Defusing guilt-tripping and emotional blackmail can be easier with scripts. Keep responses short, clear, and calm; avoid over-explaining. Try: "I understand you're upset, but I need to make this decision for myself," or "I'm not responsible for your feelings about my boundaries." If they threaten consequences, like ending the relationship, respond with, "I hope we can talk when things are calmer," and then disengage. Not reacting to drama removes the power of emotional blackmail.

When guilt creeps in, grounding yourself can help you avoid impulsive compliance. Remind yourself that setting boundaries is healthy, not cruel. You're not responsible for absorbing or solving someone else's disappointment every time you make a decision. Affirmations like "It's okay for me to say no" or "I'm allowed to put my needs first sometimes" can help anchor you and help you resist people-pleasing patterns.

Guilt-tripping often comes from those closest to you, a parent, a close friend, or a partner who knows your insecurities. The stronger the relationship, the tougher it can be to shake off old obligations. You may worry about seeming uncaring if you don't rush to help. Rehearse boundary statements in advance: "I care about our relationship, but I can't meet this request right now." Practicing or writing down these lines builds confidence.

Pay attention to your body during these situations, such as tension, stomach knots, and a lump in your throat. Physical responses often signal something's off. Trust that feeling. If helping someone always leaves you depleted while they seem unbothered, step back and protect your energy.

Unsure if a request is healthy or manipulative? Ask yourself, "Do I feel free to say no without fear?" "Is my decision respected, even if it disappoints them?" "Do they accept my boundaries without turning on me?" If not, emotional blackmail may be in play. These questions help you distinguish between authentic connection and covert control.

Standing up to guilt-tripping isn't about turning cold or cutting someone off unnecessarily; it's about refusing to be steered by fear, obligation, or shame. With practice, clarity, and self-trust, it gets easier to spot and resist emotional manipulations.

When You're Accused of Their Behavior, that's Projection and Blame-Shifting

It's a jarring experience when someone points the finger at you for something you know deep down isn't yours to own. Projection is when a toxic person accuses you of the very things they're doing themselves. Like a partner who's cheating, yet constantly suspects you of being unfaithful. Or a coworker who stirs up drama, then claims you're the one who starts conflict in the office. This isn't just bad luck or a misunderstanding.

Projection is a manipulation technique that moves their guilt, shame, or insecurity onto you, so suddenly you're the one under the microscope, defending yourself for actions that aren't even yours.

Blame-shifting works hand-in-hand with projection. A toxic person rarely takes ownership of their mistakes or poor behavior. Instead, they redirect any criticism or problem right back onto you. Imagine you point out that someone never follows through on promises. Within seconds, you're in an argument about how unreliable *you* are. You might hear, "You never appreciate what I do!" when all you did was express a need. Over time, this constant reversal can make you question your instincts and leave you wondering if you're actually the problem. The confusion is part of the plan; if you're busy defending yourself, you're not holding them accountable.

This dance of projection and blame-shifting keeps you on the defensive, constantly explaining, justifying, or apologizing for things that have little to do with your true intentions or actions. It's destabilizing. You might start to believe their accusations, or at least worry that others will. Your energy gets drained, not from solving real problems, but from running in circles against a moving target. Toxic people thrive in this chaos; it distracts everyone from their real behavior and creates an atmosphere where nobody feels safe calling out the truth.

Spotting these patterns is a critical first step in protecting yourself. Pay attention to repeated accusations that feel off-base. Do you notice a pattern where someone routinely blames you for their own habits or missteps? If so, it's probably not a coincidence. For example, if your friend constantly talks behind people's backs but then accuses *you* of gossiping every time you share a concern, that's projection. Or maybe every argument with a sibling ends with them saying *you* always start fights, when you know they've been the one picking and poking all along.

When faced with blame-shifting or projection, resist the urge to launch into long explanations or get trapped in a debate about who said what. Instead, try simple redirecting questions like, "What makes you say that?"

or "Can you give a specific example?" These questions do two things: they force the other person to slow down and clarify their accusation, and they give you space to assess whether there's any truth behind it. Often, there isn't, and their inability to provide concrete details reveals the projection for what it is: a smokescreen.

Mentally returning the projection is another powerful tool. It means quietly acknowledging to yourself that what you're being accused of isn't yours to carry. Practice grounding exercises when you feel attacked, take three deep breaths, and remind yourself where you are and what *you* know to be true. Affirmative self-talk can make a world of difference: say to yourself, "I know my intentions and actions," or "Their words don't define my reality." These statements help anchor your sense of self when someone else is determined to shake it loose.

Keep brief records of conversations where blame-shifting is frequent, just a note on your phone or in your journal after heated moments. Over time, these notes help reveal ongoing patterns and remind you that the problems aren't coming from you alone. It's easy to lose sight of reality in the moment; having a record can bring much-needed clarity.

You might even develop a mental boundary, a simple rule that says, "I'm responsible for my choices, not theirs." When accusations fly, repeat this quietly to yourself. With practice, it gets easier to hold onto your truth and refuse to pick up someone else's baggage.

The big picture here is about reclaiming your peace of mind and sense of fairness. Manipulation thrives in confusion; your clarity is your shield. By spotting projection and blame-shifting early, by using redirecting questions, grounding yourself in your reality, and resisting unnecessary self-defense, you take back control over what stories stick to you.

As we wrap up this chapter on manipulation tactics, remember. None of these behaviors is your fault, and you don't have to accept blame for things that aren't yours. Spotting subtle moves like projection lets you guard your sanity and stay grounded in what's true for you. Next up, we'll look at how your own triggers and vulnerabilities can play a role, and how learning your patterns can help to protect your boundaries even more powerfully.

Chapter Three

Mapping Your Personal Triggers and Vulnerabilities

Why You Keep Attracting Toxic People

Ever get that sinking déjà vu, like you're stuck attracting the same draining types? You meet someone, things start well, but soon enough, you're walking on eggshells or doing emotional gymnastics to keep the peace. Suppose you catch yourself wondering why this cycle keeps repeating. In that case, it's not just bad luck or deep patterns, often rooted in early relationships, that are at work.

Our blueprints for closeness, conflict, and trust form in childhood. Suppose caregivers were unpredictable, sometimes warm, sometimes cold, or critical. In that case, you may have learned to seek approval or chase elusive love. Growing up watching boundaries being ignored and disrespect being tolerated can unconsciously set that as your 'normal'. Thus, creating patterns that echo your past, even if they cause anxiety or exhaustion.

Attachment theory helps explain this. Those with anxious attachment crave closeness but fear abandonment, often ignoring the red flags to avoid being alone. People with avoidant styles protect themselves by staying guarded, attracting partners who push limits or demand too much. Suppose you played the "fixer" at home, helping siblings or smoothing over parents' moods. In that case, you may develop a chronic need to rescue others. These aren't personality flaws; they began as survival strategies but can now make you accept too much and settle for too little.

Low self-worth quietly fuels these cycles. If you believe you must earn love through sacrifice, or aren't worthy of more, you'll tolerate what should be unacceptable. Toxic people sense this; they seek those who overextend for validation. If saying no feels selfish or scary, you're at greater risk of being taken advantage of. It's not that you want chaos; chaos feels familiar.

This cycle often gets reinforced. Maybe you tried speaking up as a child and were punished, ignored, or met with gossip at work. Your brain learns: play it safe, don't make waves. Over time, you're primed for relationships where people expect compliance, and you may avoid those who'd actually honor your boundaries.

To break this cycle, map your own history. Listing your recent close relationships and noting recurring themes can help you see your progress and foster hope for change, both of which are vital to your motivation.

Journaling Your Relationship Pattern

Write about three to five significant relationships. For each, ask:

- What first attracted you?

- How did they react when you set boundaries?

- What roles did you play during conflict?

- How did you feel at your best and worst?

Look for repeating themes:

- Are you always rescuing, being the "strong one," or tiptoeing around moods?

- Where do these patterns echo earlier experiences?

The key takeaway is that these cycles aren't personal failings, but predictable results of old experiences and hidden wounds. Recognizing this can help you feel understood and less alone in your journey.

Consider Carla, a reader who realized all her boyfriends were emotionally unavailable. After journaling her relationship history, she spotted her pattern of pursuing distant partners. Instead, she began investing in friendships that reciprocated her care. She shifted from self-blame to asking, "Does this person really see me? Am I giving more than I'm getting?" With awareness, her world and relationships were transformed.

You aren't doomed to repeat these cycles. Understanding why toxic people seem familiar gives you back power and choice. Instead of repeating patterns on autopilot, you can actively choose connections that nourish and respect you. This isn't about guilt; it's about self-understanding and building better, healthier bonds.

Identifying Your Own Emotional Triggers

Emotional triggers are the invisible buttons people push, sometimes on purpose, sometimes by accident. Triggers spark strong reactions inside you. These aren't random mood swings. They're deep, automatic responses tied to old wounds or memories. You might notice your heart racing, your face getting hot, or a sudden urge to defend yourself. For example, you may freeze up or get defensive when someone criticizes you, even if it's mild. Or you find yourself panicking when someone gives you the silent treatment, because it reminds you of past rejection. Triggers are like mental tripwires; one wrong move, and suddenly you're reliving old pain.

Toxic people have a sixth sense for these triggers. They know exactly what to say or do to get a reaction. Maybe it's a snide remark about your competence, a joke at your expense in front of others, or a guilt-laced sigh when you try to set a limit. Even small gestures, a rolled eye, a dismissive shrug, can send you spiraling when they hit a sensitive spot from your past. Recognizing these triggers helps you gain clarity and control rather than blaming yourself for your reactions.

Finding your top triggers isn't about blaming yourself; it's about gaining clarity. Start by thinking back to times when someone "got under your skin" so fast you didn't even see it coming. Maybe your partner's criticism of your parenting sent you into a tailspin of anxiety. Or perhaps your boss's disappointment made you work late to avoid feeling like a failure. Write down three to five moments where your reaction felt too big for the situation. Next to each one, jot down what you were feeling, such as anger, shame, panic, worthlessness, and the story that popped into your mind. Was it "I'm letting everyone down" or "I have to fix this, or I'll be abandoned"? This exercise isn't comfortable, but it's eye-opening.

Ask yourself: What do I fear most in relationships? Is it rejection, abandonment, criticism, or being ignored? Your answers reveal patterns that toxic people may use against you, often without you even realizing it until it's too late. The real power comes from seeing the loop: A trigger gets activated (someone criticizes you), then comes your automatic response (over-explaining, apologizing, shutting down), and finally the aftermath (resentment, exhaustion, or regret). The more you become aware of this loop, the less control it has over you.

Learning to spot this trigger-response sequence helps break the cycle of automatic reactions. If you catch yourself snapping back or shutting down out of habit, pause and ask: "What am I really reacting to? Is this about now, or is it touching something old?" This moment of self-reflection interrupts the loop, allowing you to choose a different response. Instead of over-explaining or apologizing to smooth things over, you can breathe and ground yourself in the present.

Simple grounding tools work wonders in these moments. Try this: When you feel triggered, take a slow breath in for four counts, hold for four, then release for six counts. Repeat until your pulse slows a bit. If your mind is racing, look around and name five things you can see, four things you can touch, three sounds you hear, two scents you notice, and one thing you taste. This "5-4-3-2-1" grounding trick snaps your brain out of panic mode and back into reality.

Another tool is "name it to tame it." When a trigger flares up, say out loud or in your mind, "That's my fear of criticism talking." Or "This is my anxiety about being ignored." Naming the feeling puts distance between you and the reaction. It reminds you that feelings are not facts; they're signals from old stories that might no longer fit your life.

Over time, the more often you use these grounding tools and name your own triggers, the stronger your sense of control becomes. You're no longer at the mercy of every jab or guilt trip someone throws at you. Instead of spiraling into self-doubt or shame when someone pushes your buttons, you can pause, breathe, and choose how to respond. The goal isn't to be triggered; it's to learn that triggers don't have to rule your relationships anymore.

Scripts for Saying No to Break Free from People-Pleasing

People-pleasing is a sneaky habit that takes root deep, often without you realizing it. Most folks start out as kids, learning that it's safest to keep the peace, make others happy, and avoid rocking the boat at all costs. Maybe you grew up in a house where saying no meant anger or cold shoulders. Perhaps you watched a parent always bend over backward for everyone else, never for themselves. That fear of rejection clings on, whispering, "If I say no, I'll be left behind." As adults, this shows up everywhere, agreeing to extra projects at work, hosting holiday dinners you secretly dread, or saying yes to late-night phone calls when you want to rest. The truth is, people-pleasing is about survival, not kindness. It's a shield against conflict and an attempt to guarantee acceptance.

Saying no feels loaded for people-pleasers because it threatens the invisible contract they've lived by: "If I meet everyone's needs, I'll stay safe and loved." The thought of letting someone down triggers anxiety. But here's what often gets missed: saying yes to everything means saying no to yourself every time. It drains your energy, time, and even your self-respect. If you find yourself resenting commitments, avoiding certain people, or burning out, that's your inner voice begging for change.

Scripts make the scary business of saying no less daunting. With practice, they become tools you can reach for in moments of panic or guilt. In family situations, you might say, "I won't be able to make it this weekend, but I hope you all have a great time." When a coworker drops another task on your plate: "I'm at capacity and can't take on more right now." For friends pushing for plans when you need a break: "Thank you for thinking of me, but I need to pass." These aren't excuses; they're clear boundaries stated with kindness. If someone pushes back, stay calm and repeat your answer if needed. You don't owe anyone an essay or apology for protecting your own peace.

Building confidence with "no" starts in low-stakes settings. Try declining a small favor from an acquaintance or passing on an event you're not excited about. Each time you do it, notice how your anxiety flares and then fades. These are safe spaces to practice before tackling more complex situations, such as family or work. The first few times may feel awkward or even wrong, but discomfort is part of the process. It's like strengthening a muscle that's been ignored for years.

After asserting a boundary, the emotional aftermath can hit hard. Guilt and anxiety are old reflexes for people-pleasers. You might replay the conversation in your head: Did I sound rude? Will they be mad? What if they never ask me again? That rush of worry is usual, but it doesn't mean you did something wrong. In fact, it's proof that you're breaking free from patterns built up over a lifetime.

Self-compassion is crucial after standing your ground. Instead of judging yourself, pause and acknowledge the courage it took to speak up. Try this exercise: Put your hand over your heart and say (out loud if you can), "I'm allowed to take care of myself. It's okay if someone is disappointed." This simple act tells your brain that safety isn't tied to endless giving. Or grab a journal and use this prompt: "What did I fear would happen when I said no? What actually happened?" Write out both answers without editing yourself. Most times, the fallout is much less dramatic than your mind predicted.

You might also notice that some people respect you more when you say no; your boundaries reveal self-respect and confidence. The ones who push back the hardest are usually those who benefited most from your constant yes. Their discomfort isn't yours to fix.

The journey away from people-pleasing is bumpy and full of second-guessing. But each small "no" is a declaration that your needs matter too. Over time, as you practice and reflect, saying no stops feeling selfish and starts feeling like freedom. When guilt shows up again (and it will), return to compassion, remind yourself that genuine relationships can withstand honesty, and that absolute acceptance doesn't require self-sacrifice at every turn.

How Guilt and Obligation Are Used Against You

Guilt is a favorite tool of toxic people. While healthy guilt helps you own up to honest mistakes and empathize with others, toxic guilt creeps in when you've done nothing wrong but are made to feel at fault. This type of guilt arises when someone wants you to believe their needs and wants are your responsibility, leading you to sacrifice your well-being to keep the peace.

Consider situations when you felt obligated to attend a family event despite exhaustion, fearing accusations of selfishness, or agreed to favors for a friend who rarely reciprocates. That uncomfortable feeling isn't a healthy responsibility; it's imposed guilt designed to manipulate you. Manipulators are adept at using guilt and obligation; they remind you of their sacrifices or point out your perceived failures to make you comply, expecting you'll eventually give in to say yes, to relieve the pressure.

Common examples illustrate this: A mother saying, "I gave up everything for you, and this is how you repay me?" creates immediate feelings of inadequacy and a desperate urge to prove your gratitude, regardless of her unrealistic expectations. Or, a partner might list times they tolerated your flaws as ammo when you seek time for yourself, making you feel guilty not for your actions, but for not meeting their current demands. Over time, your own happiness starts to feel like a debt you can never repay.

Recognizing when guilt is used as a weapon is crucial. Toxic people excel at framing their requests as moral obligations, using phrases like "After all I've done for you," "I would do it for you," or "No one else would put up with this." The message? Not doing what they want makes you a failure in your role. The truth: Their wants are not automatically your responsibilities.

Spotting and Challenging False Guilt

Identifying "false guilt" is essential for reclaiming your boundaries. Think it over for a moment and ask yourself: Is this guilt rooted in my values or someone else's expectations? Did I truly harm anyone, or am I just being told I did? Would I expect a friend to feel guilty here? If the answer is no, then the guilt may not be yours to carry.

Query, when guilt arises:

- Did I willingly agree to this?

- Is this request fair and reasonable?

- Would I feel this pressure if someone else asked?

- Am I prioritizing their feelings over my own well-being?

This mental checklist helps you distinguish legitimate responsibility from manipulation.

Useful Scripts and Mental Reframes

Scripts and affirmations can deflect guilt trips. If someone says, "I thought I could count on you," try: "I understand this is important to you, but I'm not able to help." Affirm to yourself: "My needs matter too," or "It's okay if someone is disappointed." Prioritizing your well-being is not selfish; it's necessary.

Sometimes, stating the simple truth is enough: "I appreciate your feelings, but I have to take care of myself right now," or, "I hear you're upset, but I can't do that." This might feel uncomfortable at first because toxic guilt tricks you into thinking self-care is betrayal. With practice, these responses become robust defenses.

Changing Your Perspective on Disappointment

A vital mental shift is understanding that causing disappointment isn't catastrophic; everyone experiences it. Adults have the right to say no without being villains. You aren't responsible for managing everyone else's emotions or rescuing them from discomfort. When old guilt patterns echo in your mind, "You're ungrateful," "You never do enough," pause and ask: Would I say this to a friend? If not, don't say it to yourself.

Healthy connections include respect for each other's limits. If saying no always makes you feel like the bad guy, that's not mutual care, it's manipulation masked as love. The more you build boundaries and reject artificial obligation, the more freedom and lightness you'll find in your life.

Reclaiming Self-Trust After Gaslighting and Manipulation

If you've spent months or years with someone who constantly twists your words, denies your experiences, or insists their version of events is the only truth, you know the quiet torment of doubting your own reality. Gaslighting and chronic manipulation can batter your self-trust until everyday choices become stressful puzzles. You could stand in the middle of the kitchen, second-guessing where you put your keys. Or you replay conversations, wondering if you misheard or overreacted. Even simple decisions, what to eat, which route to take to work, who to trust with a secret, can fill you with uncertainty. You might hear yourself thinking, "Did that really happen the way I remember?" or "Am I being too dramatic?" Over time, this gnaws at your confidence, making you hesitant to speak up or act without reassurance.

The effects linger because manipulation seeps deep into your thought patterns. Little by little, you may start relying on others to confirm what you saw, heard, or felt. Self-doubt grows as you look outside yourself for permission and validation. This isn't just forgetfulness; it's a learned habit of mistrusting your own inner compass. It's common for survivors of gaslighting to feel lost or unmoored, as if their instincts have been scrambled.

But there's good news: self-trust is not gone forever. It just needs nurturing, patience, and some new habits to wake it up again. One of the first steps is building a daily "reality check" routine. Start by writing down a few details from your day, what happened, how you felt, and what you noticed about your mood or thoughts. This simple act gives you proof of your own reality, especially when doubts creep in later. You might jot down, "Had coffee with Sarah at noon, laughed about the dog video she showed me," or "Felt tense after that meeting, my stomach tightened when my manager raised her voice." This isn't about being right or wrong; it's about reconnecting with your experiences.

Another helpful practice is making a list each evening called "Three things I know for sure." They don't need to be profound. You might write, "I made my bed this morning," "I called my sister after work," or "I felt proud when I finished that project." This daily ritual helps anchor you in facts and feelings that are yours alone. Over time, these small acts of self-validation chip away at the old script that says you can't trust your memory or judgment.

As your confidence grows in these private routines, begin challenging yourself with small decisions in daily life. Pick a new café for lunch without polling friends first. Plan an afternoon outing based on what interests you, not just what others want. If a friend asks where to meet up, suggest a spot without apologizing or hedging. These are low-stakes choices, but each one is a workout for your decision-making muscles. Notice how it feels to choose and stick with it, even if it's something as minor as which movie to watch on a Saturday night.

For many people, rebuilding self-trust, progress unfolds in tiny victories. One day, you realize you trusted your gut about a coworker's intentions, and later you learn you were right. You may notice you're not checking and rechecking every text before hitting send. A reader named Luis once shared how he finally chose a new haircut without asking five people for their opinions first, then celebrated by taking a selfie and sending it only to himself. That small win mattered more than any outside praise.

When you slip back into old habits (it happens) and seek reassurance or doubt yourself, don't beat yourself up. Recovery isn't a straight line; it's more like a dance with a few steps forward and some back. The fact that you're noticing these patterns means healing is happening.

Here's a gentle reminder: rebuilding trust in yourself takes time and kindness. You might have days when doubt feels overwhelming, and others when clarity breaks through like sunshine after rain. Each moment of self-awareness and every small choice made on your own terms is proof that your inner compass still works.

As we close this chapter, remember the work you're doing now lays the foundation for stronger boundaries and more confident choices ahead. Trusting yourself again is possible, step by step. In the next chapter, we'll move from inner work to practical strategies for setting boundaries and protecting your peace, even when others push back hard.

Chapter Four

Setting Boundaries Without Guilt

The Science of Boundaries and Why They Work

Think of your life as a garden. You want your happiness and sense of self to flourish. A fence around your garden isn't about being unfriendly; it's about protecting what matters. Boundaries act as a fence, defining where you end, and others begin, keeping your well-being safe while still allowing connection. Without any fence, problems creep in, and you may feel overwhelmed or drained. If the fence is too high, you shut everyone out. The real skill is finding the middle ground, a fence sturdy enough to keep out harm but low enough to let you enjoy warmth and community.

Boundaries are your psychological "property lines." They're not punishments or isolation strategies. Instead, they clarify where your feelings and needs end, and another's begin. With healthy boundaries, you decide who helps or affects you, and how much you tend to others. Boundaries let you say yes or no authentically. These aren't just preferences; they're critical for emotional health. Research from UC Davis Health shows that clear boundaries protect mental safety, prevent burnout, and add essential structure to relationships (UC Davis Health, 2024, March 13).

Your brain benefits from clear boundaries. Neuroscience confirms that setting limits, such as turning off work notifications or declining last-minute plans, lowers stress hormones. The amygdala, a part of the brain that manages stress, relaxes in a sense of safety. People who set boundaries have higher self-esteem and less anxiety and resentment. Boundaries aren't about keeping others out; they're also about valuing your needs.

There are three main types of boundaries: rigid, porous, and healthy. Think of them as three kinds of fences. Rigid boundaries can turn into fortress walls; you rarely share, refuse help, and avoid vulnerability, leading to disconnection. Porous boundaries are more like broken fences; you say yes involuntarily, absorb others' problems, and struggle to protect your time and energy, often resulting in exhaustion or resentment. For example, a rigid boundary might be refusing to discuss feelings, while a porous one might be always saying yes to social invitations, even when overwhelmed. Healthy boundaries are balanced, allowing flexibility and protection.

Healthy boundaries are balanced. They resemble a sturdy picket fence, not too high, not too weak. You can share openly but selectively, help others without self-sacrifice, and say no confidently and guilt-free. If anyone crosses your line, you can gently but firmly reset it. This approach enables you to feel more in control and confident in managing your relationships.

Healthy Boundary Review

- Boundary Type Description Example Rigid Wall-like; excludes most; keeps everyone out "I don't talk about my feelings, ever."

- Porous-Loose; little protection; lets everything and everyone in "I always say yes, even when overwhelmed."

- Healthy-Balanced; lets in good, keeps out harm; flexible but sturdy. "I'd love to help, but I need downtime."

You might think setting boundaries is "mean" or selfish. But saying no to others is saying yes to yourself, a healthy, vital act. Boundaries are being respectful to everyone. They prevent confusion and resentment by setting clear expectations. When you place a limit kindly and directly, you empower others to do the same.

Many of us have been conditioned to think that setting limits is rude or uncaring, especially if we grew up in a culture that expected self-sacrifice. Guilt often surfaces when we start prioritizing ourselves. The truth is, boundaries are a gift. They allow for clarity and honesty, so no one has to guess your needs or feel anxious about overstepping. When you better understand your own needs, setting boundaries becomes a natural act of self-respect and compassion. Genuine compassion includes honoring your own needs alongside others'. Setting boundaries isn't shutting people out; it's inviting more genuine, respectful interactions.

Boundaries also shift as relationships and needs change (UC Davis Health, 2024, March 13). Just as a garden fence may need repairs after a storm or expansion for new flowers, your limits can be adjusted after significant life events or stressful periods.

If you catch yourself hesitating to set a boundary out of fear of appearing cold, remember: protecting your well-being is healthy for everyone involved. When you care for your own garden first, you have more energy and joy to share with everyone else.

"My Garden Fence"

Take a few quiet minutes. Visualize your life as a fenced garden:

- Who holds the keys to the gate?

- Where are the weak spots?

- Where is the fence too high or in need of repair?

Identify one area (work, home, friends) where your boundary feels weak, and write down a step you'll take this week to make it stronger.

How to Set Boundaries with a Toxic Parent Without Family Fallout

The thought of setting boundaries with a parent can feel like carrying a live wire, one wrong move and the sparks fly everywhere. To navigate this, prepare a calm, clear message beforehand, such as, 'I need some space to focus on my work,' or 'I can't take calls during dinner.' Use 'I' statements to express your feelings without blame. It's not just about rules or schedules; it's about years of expectation, guilt, and the invisible weight of 'good child' programming stitched into your bones. Many people wrestle with the fear that if they say no to a parent, whether it's shutting down those daily marathon phone calls or refusing to drop everything for another last-minute request, they'll trigger hurt feelings, angry texts, or whispers among siblings. Sometimes, the hardest part isn't even the parents' reaction but your own tidal wave of guilt and second-guessing. Remember, setting boundaries is a process, not a one-time event, and consistency helps build understanding over time.

Picture someone in their late thirties, juggling work, kids, and a needy mom who calls before breakfast, after lunch, and again at bedtime. Each call is loaded with complaints or requests for favors. The adult child tries to explain that they need more space, but every attempt ends with the parent sighing, "I guess I just won't bother you anymore." Soon, even thinking about saying no sparks dread. This is how old family roles box us in: you're the helper, the fixer, the "good one." Breaking out feels like breaking a promise.

The first step is to identify with crystal clarity what you need. It could be fewer calls, no more unannounced visits, or limits on lending money. Write it down in plain language: "I can't do daily calls," "I need notice before visits," or "I'm not able to lend money anymore." The more specific, the easier it is to stick to when pressure mounts. Next, plan how you'll deliver this message, choose a calm moment when you're not already on edge. Decide whether a phone call, face-to-face talk, or even a text fits best for your situation and comfort level. Practice your words if needed. Imagine possible reactions so you're not blindsided in the moment.

When it's time to communicate, keep your tone warm but firm. Use precise language and focus on your needs, not their flaws. For example: "Mom, I love talking to you, but I need to limit our calls to twice a week so I have time for my family and myself." Or, "Dad, it helps me when you let me know before stopping by, I can't do drop-ins anymore." If money is the issue: "I'm not able to help financially right now, I need to stick to my own budget." Short sentences work best; don't over-explain or apologize for having needs.

Scripts that can help steady you in the moment

- "I value our relationship, but I also need time for myself."

- "I'm not able to come by today."

- "I'm happy to talk this weekend instead of every day."

- "I care about you, but I can't help with that right now."

Pushback is almost guaranteed. Some parents will guilt-trip or escalate, "You're so ungrateful," or, "After all I've done for you..." Others may triangulate by pulling in siblings, "Your brother never treats me like this," or start gossiping to other relatives. When this happens, resist the urge to debate or defend at length. Use a quick response: "I appreciate all you've done for me, but this is what I need right now." Or, "I'm not discussing this with others; it's between us." Stick to your limit and repeat as needed; consistency is key.

Managing sibling alliances can get tricky fast. If your brother or sister calls on behalf of your parent and says, "Mom says you never help out anymore," respond: "I'm working out my relationship with Mom directly." Don't let yourself get sucked into old family triangles or defense sprees.

If family gossip swirls ("Everyone thinks you're being harsh"), remember that others may not understand your boundaries because they benefit from the status quo. You don't owe them an explanation. You can say, "This decision is right for me even if others disagree."

Handling escalation means staying calm even when drama rises. If a parent hangs up, sends angry messages, or tries emotional blackmail ("You'll regret treating me this way"), avoid reacting in kind. Give space if emotions run high. Return later with a steady message: "I hope we can talk when things are calmer."

Holding boundaries with a parent isn't about punishment; it's about protecting your well-being and building a healthier relationship. Expect some bumps along the way, and keep your eyes on what you need in the long term. Over time, most parents adjust, even if they never fully accept your limits, because consistency and calm eventually win out over chaos and guilt.

Scripts for Enforcing Boundaries at Work (Even with a Difficult Boss)

Setting boundaries at work can feel risky, especially if your boss is unpredictable or coworkers challenge your limits. Workplace power dynamics and your professional reputation can make you fear being seen as "difficult" or risking your position. However, there's an essential distinction between assertiveness and insubordination: the former is about clearly and respectfully stating your needs or limits, while the latter means refusing reasonable requests or being disrespectful. The key lies in your tone, timing, and word choice; you can advocate for yourself while remaining professional.

It's helpful to have scripts ready for tricky situations. When your boss gives you more work at 5 p.m. on a Friday, try: "I'm happy to help.

Can you share the deadline and priorities so I can manage my current projects?" This signals cooperation without passively accepting unrealistic loads. If a coworker pries into your personal life or seems intent on gossiping, you can respond, "I prefer to keep my personal life private, but thanks for asking." For after-hours emails or texts, set a simple limit: "I'm unavailable after 6 p.m., but I'll respond in the morning." If someone makes jokes or comments that cross a line, be direct: "That comment made me uncomfortable." This clarifies that you've noticed and won't accept it.

When speaking with those higher up, carefully select your words: "I'd like to discuss my current workload before taking on new assignments." With direct reports, clarity is essential: "I expect updates by Tuesday, so we stay on track," or "Let me know if you need help prioritizing tasks." With peers, be friendly but firm: "I can join the project meeting, but will need an agenda in advance so I can prepare." Adjusting your tone and message to the audience you're addressing can maintain productivity and reduce friction.

Example Power Up & Power Down Scripts

Boss/Supervisor Relationship:

- **Power Up**: "Could we clarify which projects take priority right now?"

- **Power Down**: "I'm at capacity. What should I pause to fit this in?"

Peer Relationship:

- **Power Up**: "Let's set clear roles, so work isn't duplicated."

- **Power Down**: "I'm happy to help once I've finished my assigned tasks."

Subordinate Relationship:

- **Power Up**: "Let's agree on deadlines and touch base weekly."

- **Power Down**: "If you need help, please ask sooner rather than later."

Professionalism is essential. You don't need to justify your boundaries with lengthy explanations or apologies. Stay neutral and succinct. If someone resists, restate your point or ask for clarification: "Can you clarify which task is the top priority?" You're not being stubborn, you're clarifying expectations.

Sometimes, setting boundaries alone isn't enough, especially if a boss or colleague keeps pushing or crosses the line into harassment. In these situations, document what happened (dates, times, what was said or done, and your response). For digital requests, such as late-night emails, reply in writing that you'll respond during business hours. This not only reinforces your boundary but also creates a record of it.

If behavior doesn't improve, you may need to involve HR or management. When reporting, stick to the facts: "I've addressed this issue with [Name] several times, but it continues." Present your documentation without exaggeration. Clear records show you're serious and objective.

It's normal to feel anxious about setting workplace boundaries, especially if past experiences have made you wary. Yet, not setting boundaries can lead to stress, resentment, burnout, or repeated exploitation. Practicing your scripts in lower-stakes situations helps build confidence for bigger ones. Over time, assertive boundary-setting becomes part of your professional identity, and you're seen as reliable, transparent, and self-respecting.

Remember, you have the right to protect your time, energy, and dignity at work. Boundaries demonstrate that you value yourself and expect respect from others; they don't make you a troublemaker.

Know When to Set Limits and When to Walk Away In Navigating Friendships

Friendships can become tricky when you feel things aren't right anymore. You might notice you're the one always reaching out, listening, or doing favors. At the same time, your friend only contacts you when they need something or often vents for hours, then disappears when you talk about your own problems. Sometimes the imbalance appears slowly. Maybe your friend disguises put-downs as jokes, cancels plans at the last minute without apology, or reveals your secrets for amusement. If you start dreading their messages or feel drained after spending time together, that's a sign that something is off. Friendships should feel balanced, not one-sided.

There are clear warning signs that a friendship is turning toxic. If you're stuck in a pattern where your needs, time, or boundaries are regularly overlooked, pay attention. Manipulation can appear subtly, such as guilt-tripping you for saying no, turning others against you, or taking advantage of your kindness. Disrespect is another red flag, such as belittling your successes or life choices under the guise of honesty. If these behaviors show up, trust your instincts; healthy friendships build you up, not break you down.

Checklist of Friendship Red Flags

- You feel anxious before spending time with them.
- Conversations mostly spotlight their issues.
- Your boundaries get minimized or dismissed.
- They try to one-up you or compete with you.
- You feel worse about yourself after seeing them.

- Your feelings are dismissed, or you're made to doubt your memory.

- They gossip about you or others.

- Rare apologies, frequent blame.

If any of these happen, it's time to consider setting limits. Saying no to a friend can feel tough, especially if you care about them, but preserving your energy is essential. Try, "I care about you, but I can't talk every night," or, "I need more space in my schedule." If they constantly unload their problems, say, "I don't have the capacity for a deep conversation tonight." When you feel obligated rather than excited about invitations, it's okay to decline: "Thanks, but I'm taking downtime this weekend." These scripts might feel uncomfortable at first, but each honest response strengthens your boundaries and the relationship.

Friends may push back when you start asserting your boundaries, especially if they're used to you always saying yes. They could act hurt or accuse you of changing. Stay calm, restate your limit, and know that you don't owe anyone an elaborate explanation; a simple "I need this right now" suffices. If the friendship can't handle boundaries, it may not be as strong as you thought.

Sometimes, boundaries aren't enough. If patterns of manipulation or disrespect continue, you should step back further or end the friendship. It's difficult to walk away from someone who mattered, but protecting your well-being sometimes requires tough choices. If you decide to part ways, communicate clearly and kindly: "Our friendship isn't feeling healthy for me right now, so I need to step back." Focus on your own feelings and what you need, without rehashing every issue.

The aftermath of ending a friendship can be painful. Grief over a lost friendship can feel as intense as a breakup, with memories resurfacing unexpectedly. You may even second-guess your decision. Be gentle with yourself; this pain means the friendship was meaningful and that you're growing.

Self-compassion is crucial. Allow yourself to mourn the good while recognizing what didn't work. Journaling can help process your feelings and clarify what you've learned. Ask yourself, "What did this experience teach me about my needs and boundaries?" The insights may surprise you.

Building new support systems helps. List people who uplift and energize you; it might be a long-lost friend, a supportive coworker, or a group you share interests with. Reach out intentionally and nurture these positive connections. When you let go of toxic friendships, your social network can evolve in healthier, more fulfilling ways.

Letting go is never easy, but honoring your boundaries creates room for better, more reciprocal friendships in your life.

How to Handle Pushback or What to Do When Boundaries Trigger Backlash

Setting boundaries with someone who is used to getting their way rarely goes smoothly at first. One of the most common reactions to finally saying "no" is immediate and often dramatic resistance, guilt trips, angry outbursts, or the silent treatment. This is especially tough when you're new to standing up for yourself. For example, telling a parent you can't run errands every weekend might get you labeled selfish, be met with reminders of past sacrifices, or spark a campaign to involve other family members. This backlash can make it tempting to slip back into old patterns, but it's not failure. It's a sign your boundary is working, and the other person is testing whether you'll hold firm.

Toxic individuals are particularly adept at seeking out your vulnerabilities to pull you back into old routines. While backlash is uncomfortable, it shows you're shifting the power dynamic. When you expect some escalation, that helps you feel more prepared rather than caught off guard.

When reactions are intense, de-escalation is key. Emotional outbursts can be overwhelming, but you don't need to match that energy. Use the "broken record" technique: calmly and kindly repeat your boundary, no matter their protests. If a parent pleads, "But I need you this weekend," repeat, "I understand that's hard, but I won't be available." If they get loud or argumentative, respond evenly, "I've said what I can do. I hope you understand." Don't get drawn into defending yourself; stick to your phrase, repeat as needed, and avoid extra explanations.

For silent treatment or withdrawal (classic manipulation), resist the urge to chase, apologize, or try to fix things. Let the silence sit. Although it feels uncomfortable, often the best response is to do nothing. If triangulation occurs, like a sibling reaching out to tell you how upset your parent is, don't engage in the drama. Say neutrally, "I'm working things out directly with her." Don't explain yourself or try to recruit allies.

It's normal to feel discomfort and anxiety the first few times you stand firm. The urge to give in will be strong. Your nervous system craves relief from tension. Visualization can help: imagine yourself as a surfer riding a wave of discomfort. The urge to retreat will peak and then subside if you don't react impulsively. Remind yourself of "It's okay if someone is upset by my boundary." Their reaction is their responsibility. Each time you stay solid under pressure, your confidence grows.

In some cases, backlash may escalate further, showing up as threats, intense hostility, or attempts to isolate you. This is when safety and support matter most. Identify one person you trust, a friend, a therapist, or a support group, who understands why your boundaries matter and can support you when things get heated. Reach out before and after tough conversations. If you encounter harassment, like repeated texts, unwanted visits, or threats, document everything (dates, times, and actions). If you feel unsafe or experience stalking or harassment, don't hesitate to contact authorities or professionals.

Taking care of yourself is crucial. Self-care isn't just relaxation; it's taking space from your phone, going for a walk, journaling, or reminding yourself why your boundaries matter. Preserve your peace and energy; defending your boundaries is not selfish; it's essential.

Backlash doesn't mean you're doing it wrong. It means change is happening. Responding to pushback calmly builds your skills, and, over time, people learn your limits aren't negotiable. Protecting your boundaries keeps relationships honest and preserves your well-being, even if things are messy at first.

Next, we'll explore how to heal and rebuild your self-worth after years of toxic patterns, so you can thrive, and not just survive, in all areas of your life.

Chapter Five

Communication Blueprints for Difficult Conversations

Assertive Communication or How to Speak Up Without Fear

There's a moment most of us know well: you rehearse what you want to say, your heart pounds, and then, when the time comes, you either say nothing or blurt out words you regret. You may be at work, steeling yourself to address a colleague's constant interruptions. Or you're at home, struggling to tell a relative you can't drop everything for their latest request. The fear of backlash, awkward silence, or being labeled 'difficult' can make anyone second-guess speaking up. Yet, staying silent often leaves you simmering with resentment, while going on the attack can blow up a conversation before it even starts. The challenge is finding that steady, confident middle ground, assertiveness, where you can voice what matters to you without bulldozing others or shrinking away. This section provides practical strategies to help you communicate confidently and handle difficult conversations effectively.

Assertive communication is not about dominating a conversation or making demands. It's simply expressing your needs, feelings, and rights with clarity and respect, standing up for yourself while recognizing the dignity of the other person. Let's clear up some confusion: assertiveness isn't aggression (which bulldozes and blames), nor is it passivity (which swallows your needs). And it's definitely not passive-aggression, that old favorite where frustration leaks out in sarcasm or icy silence. Using respectful language can help you feel safer and more respected, making it easier to stay calm and open during tough talks.

How do you actually practice being assertive when stress is high, and your brain wants to freeze or flee? A step-by-step approach can help. First, plan your message: What do you really want to communicate? Boil it down to one or two key points to stay focused. Next, use the "State, Wait, Repeat" technique. Start by calmly stating your need or concern: "I need my time after work to recharge." Then pause, let your words settle, without rushing to fill the silence, even if it feels uncomfortable. If the other person ignores you or steamrolls you, repeat your message: "I understand you want help tonight, but I'm not available." This can help you feel more in control and less overwhelmed during conflicts.

A super useful tool here is the "I feel...when...because...I need..." template. For example: "I feel disrespected when my ideas are dismissed in meetings because collaboration matters to me. I need my contributions to be considered." This format keeps blame out of the equation and centers the conversation on facts and needs rather than accusations. If you're declining a demand, you can use: "I'm not able to do that," without piling on excuses or apologies. Clear, brief language carries authority and confidence.

When it's time actually to have the tough conversation, scripts can be a lifesaver. Here are a couple you can keep in your back pocket: If someone's tone gets nasty or personal, try: "I need our conversations to stay respectful, or I'll have to step away." When you need to decline a request, whether it's overtime at work or a social invite you can't handle, use: "I'm not able to do that." If pressed for reasons, resist the pressure to over-explain; repeating your answer calmly is enough.

Your words matter, but how you say them is just as important. Calm confidence comes from steady body language and even breathing. Stand or sit upright without crossing your arms or fidgeting. Maintain steady but kind eye contact, not a stare-down, and keep your voice level. If anxiety creeps in, focus on controlled breathing: inhale slowly for four counts, hold for two, then exhale for six. This simple act loosens tension and gives your brain a chance to catch up with your mouth. Mastering your body language and tone helps you stay composed and assertive, even in stressful moments.

Role-Play Assertiveness With a Friend

Find a reliable friend and ask them to play the part of someone who pushes back when you set a boundary. Use the 'State, Wait, Repeat' method and practice holding your ground calmly. Switch roles so you experience both sides, delivering the message and receiving it. Afterward, talk about what felt natural and what was hard.

- Did you keep eye contact?

- Did your voice stay steady?

- Where did nerves show up?

Jot down any phrases that felt strong or moments where you struggled. This exercise builds muscle memory so you're less likely to freeze or panic when it's for real. Regular practice enhances your confidence and prepares you for real-life situations, making assertiveness more natural over time.

Learning assertive communication doesn't mean every conversation will go perfectly or that toxic people will magically respect your new boundaries. But it does help you show up for yourself with dignity and clarity, which makes all the difference in protecting your peace and building healthier connections.

De-Escalating Toxic Arguments With Language That Calms Instead of Fueling the Fire

Arguments with toxic people can quickly spiral out of control. Even if you mean well, things often escalate: voices rise, old wounds are revisited, and you may feel caught in a cycle of blame or defensiveness. These interactions don't follow the guidelines of healthy conflict. Standard advice like "just talk it out" usually fails, sometimes making things worse, because toxic individuals thrive on emotional chaos. They know how to bait you, whether by referencing your past mistakes or laying on guilt. These emotional hooks lure you in, tempting you to react, justify, or fix the situation. The more you engage, the deeper the spiral.

Escalation occurs because toxic people seek control or the feeling of victory, not resolution. When emotions flare, you might argue, defend, or over-explain, which only fuels the dispute. Their goal is to keep you off balance; feeling confused or agitated makes it harder for you to stand your ground. That's why traditional conflict-resolution strategies, like clearly stating your feelings or seeking compromise, often fail with toxic people and can sometimes even escalate the conflict.

What works instead is changing your approach. Use language and actions that cool things down rather than escalate. For example, phrases like "Let's take a break and talk when we're both calmer" or "I hear that you're upset. I'm willing to listen when the conversation stays respectful" acknowledge emotions but set healthy boundaries. You're not giving in to drama, and you're not adding fuel to the fire.

Sometimes silence is more effective than words. When the conversation turns ugly or repetitive, pause before responding; an awkward silence can help defuse tension. You don't need to reply right away; let the silence cool things off. If things heat up, say, "I'm going to step outside for a few minutes; we can continue later." This break allows emotions to settle and signals you won't tolerate ongoing hostility.

Walking away isn't defeat; it's a show of self-control. Toxic people may push harder if they sense you're leaving, but consistent calmness shows you won't play their game. If the argument keeps circling back to the same accusations and no progress is being made, use firm language to end it: "We're not getting anywhere right now, so I'm going to stop this conversation."

Sometimes arguments cross the line into unsafe territory, maybe with threats, shouting, or relentless personal attacks. In these moments, prioritizing your safety is most important. Use a clear, non-negotiable exit: "I don't feel safe right now, so I'm ending this conversation." If you feel threatened, leave immediately. Your well-being comes first.

In especially volatile situations, it helps to have a safety plan. Arrange a code word (like "pineapple") with a trusted friend or family member. If you send it, they know to check on you or call for help. This kind of backup can give you added confidence in unpredictable arguments.

What To Do When Arguments Spin Out of Control

- **Conversation looping without progress**: Pause. Say, "We're going in circles. Let's take a break and revisit this later."

- **Accusations become personal attacks**: Say, "This is getting disrespectful. I'm stepping away for now."

- **Manipulation or guilt-tripping appears**: Respond, "I'm not discussing this until we can be respectful."

- **If you feel threatened or unsafe**: Use your emergency exit and leave.

- **Afterward**: Connect with your support person and document what happened while it's fresh.

When de-escalating toxic arguments, the goal isn't to win or convince the other person. Your focus is on protecting your peace and staying safe from harm or manipulation. The way you use your words and actions brings stability and control to a chaotic situation.

What to Say (And What Not to Say) When Responding to Gaslighting

You know that moment when you're halfway through a conversation and suddenly start doubting everything you just said or remembered? Gaslighting has a way of making you question your sanity, your memory, and even your worth. It's sneaky, less about wild lies and more about subtle, repeated undermining. Someone insists a conversation never happened, claims you're "always overreacting," or twists facts until you feel cornered. The trap is real: they bait you into defending yourself, explaining every detail, or arguing over who's "right" about the past. You end up exhausted, chasing your own tail, and walking away with more self-doubt than answers.

The biggest mistake most people make in these moments is trying to prove their reality to the gaslighter. You might find yourself replaying events, listing facts, or desperately searching for receipts or messages as evidence. Yet, no matter how much you explain, the other person always seems to have a comeback or a new angle. This isn't a fair debate; it's a power play designed to keep you off balance. The more you defend, the more you get tangled in their web. Avoid falling into the trap of defending every detail or arguing over who remembers what. Debates over "who's right" about past events rarely end well; instead, they drain your energy and feed the gaslighter's control.

Instead, focus on calmly asserting your own reality without getting dragged into a battle. Short, firm statements work best when you feel the conversation shifting into gaslighting territory. Try saying, "That's not how I remember it." This simple line draws a line in the sand without getting aggressive or defensive. Or use, "We see this differently, and that's okay."

You acknowledge the disagreement but refuse to spend hours justifying yourself. If you sense the conversation is going nowhere because you can't agree on what happened, set a clear conversational boundary: "If we can't agree on what happened, I'm not going to keep discussing it." This lets you opt out of pointless debates and shows that your perception is valid, no matter how much the other person pushes back.

Some people will double down when you won't play their game. They might accuse you of being stubborn, dramatic, or even dishonest. The urge to argue back or defend yourself can be strong, but resist it. Each time you answer their challenge or try to prove your point, you give them another opening. Stick with your original statement, repeat it if needed, and avoid being pulled into circular debates. Keep responses brief and neutral signals that you're not available for their games.

Detaching from gaslighting conversations doesn't mean pretending nothing happened. After an incident, take time to validate your own experience. The most powerful tool for this is a simple self-validation routine. As soon as possible after the conversation, write out exactly what happened in a journal, what was said, how you felt, and what details stick out in your memory. This log isn't for anyone else; it's for you to ground yourself in your own reality. If doubts creep in later (and they often do), reread your notes and remind yourself: "My memory and feelings are valid, even if others deny them." This affirmation helps reset your confidence and keeps the gaslighting from burrowing deeper into you.

You can also create a short mantra for moments when you feel wobbly: "I trust my perception." Use it in the heat of a conversation or afterward when self-doubt starts to gnaw at you. Talk with a trusted friend who can listen without judgment. Sometimes, hearing someone else say, "Yeah, that sounds off," can quiet your inner critic.

Remember that gaslighting works by isolating you from your own truth. It wants you to be confused and constantly second-guessing. Refusing to debate details or accept shifting stories takes away some of that power. Even if the other person never admits fault or agrees with your version of events, you can hold onto what you know to be true for yourself.

Self-Validation Journaling

Take ten minutes after any confusing conversation and jot down:

- What was said (stick to direct quotes if possible)?
- How did their words make you feel: angry, sad, or uncertain?
- What do you remember most clearly?

Revisit this log when doubts creep up or when the same person tries to twist things again.

Building this habit will slowly restore your confidence in your own memories and instincts, even if someone else spends all their energy trying to shake them loose.

Use 'Gray Rock' and Minimal Contact to Master Neutral Responses

Dealing with someone who thrives on drama or conflict, whether it's a coworker, a boundary-crossing family member, or a meddling ex, often leaves you feeling drained. Engaging with them usually fuels their behavior. The "gray rock" method offers an alternative: you need to become so emotionally neutral and uninteresting that the toxic person loses interest in you. The goal isn't to win or outsmart them; it's to remove yourself as their source of emotional energy.

The "gray rock" technique is straightforward but takes practice. When someone tries to provoke you, give bland, neutral responses. Avoid big explanations or emotional reactions. Use short, unremarkable replies: "Okay." "I see." "Thanks." "Noted." Withhold personal information, your reactions, or anything that could be used against you. Over time, when these individuals don't get the reaction they seek, they often lose interest.

Real-Life Examples

If a sibling calls only to complain or seek drama, then respond, "I see." If pressed for an opinion, say, "That's your perspective." In the workplace, if someone criticizes your project and you expect defensiveness, reply, "Okay," and move on. Initially, not defending or explaining yourself can feel awkward, but that discomfort helps create boundaries. The less you provide for them to use, the less power they have to provoke or manipulate.

Emotional Detachment

Emotionally detaching can be hard, especially if you're used to trying to fix things or feeling guilty. Try visualizing an invisible barrier, a bubble or shield, around you during interactions, letting their words bounce off. Pair this with an internal mantra like, "I don't have to react." Repeat it to yourself whenever you feel the urge to defend or engage. This helps form a mental buffer, making neutrality easier over time.

Minimal Contact Strategy

Minimal contact isn't about ignoring or ghosting someone; it's about setting deliberate boundaries that protect your peace. When you can't go no-contact (e.g., due to shared responsibilities), keep interactions brief and focused on essential matters only. Clearly limit topics to what's necessary, like schedules or finances, and avoid personal conversations. Decide in advance how long you'll interact, and stick to it.

For ongoing connections where cutting contact isn't possible, use written communication whenever you can. Texts and emails offer a natural barrier, allowing you to respond thoughtfully and keep things factual. For example, when coordinating pickups with a difficult ex: "Pick up at 4 p.m.

at school." Ignore personal jabs and stick to logistics. You don't need to respond to every message; one clear reply is enough.

Navigating Perceived Coldness

You may worry that such neutrality is rude or cold, but being emotionally neutral is often easier and healthier than being drawn into drama. With practice, it feels more natural, and toxic people will tire of trying to provoke you. The aim isn't to suppress your entire personality, but to save your energy for healthy relationships.

Safety First

If "gray rocking" seems unsafe (e.g., if someone is escalating or harassing you), prioritize your safety and seek help from trusted people or professionals. But for most day-to-day toxic interactions, with family, colleagues, or in group chats, neutral responses can be your best defense. Your emotional peace matters more than satisfying someone else's craving for a reaction.

Keep Tools Handy

Keep neutral phrases nearby, on your phone or a sticky note: "I see." "Alright." "Noted." "Thank you for letting me know." Every time you choose neutrality over arguing or explaining, note how much lighter you feel. Over time, these small changes give you back control over your emotional space, even amid chaos.

Handling Public Manipulation When Toxic People Try to Shame You in Groups

Public manipulation is its own kind of storm. There's something uniquely unsettling about being singled out or embarrassed in front of others, whether it's a workplace meeting, a family gathering, or a group of friends.

PRACTICAL WAYS TO PROTECT YOURSELF FROM TOXIC PEOPLE

Toxic people often use these settings as a stage, relying on the presence of an audience to amplify their power and put you on the spot. You might find yourself the butt of a "joke" about your work habits during a team call, or suddenly the topic of a family member's complaint at Thanksgiving. These moments sting more than private comments because the public eye adds pressure. You may feel boxed in, exposed, or unable to defend yourself without looking defensive or "too sensitive." The manipulation often takes the form of scapegoating ("If it weren't for you, this wouldn't have happened"), sly jokes at your expense, or even outright shaming, sometimes disguised as "just being honest."

What makes these situations so challenging is that you're not just dealing with the manipulator, you're also managing the crowd. There's the awkward silence, the uncertain glances, and sometimes, worst of all, the people who join in or stay quiet. The manipulator hopes you'll either laugh along and accept the jab or overreact and look unreasonable. Your best move is neither. Instead, you can use calm, clear language that calls out the behavior without raising the temperature. If someone makes a "joke" about your competence in a meeting, try saying, "That's not appropriate for this setting." It focuses on the behavior, not your feelings. If a relative starts airing grievances at a family event, reply with, "Let's discuss this privately, not in front of everyone." Short, direct phrases like these break the spell of group manipulation. They signal that you see what's happening and won't play along.

Sometimes it helps to have allies in the room. If you know in advance that a particular coworker or family member tends to stir up drama, talk with someone you trust before the event. Let them know you need backup, a simple redirect in conversation, or even a supportive presence. For example, if you're worried about being singled out at a meeting, ask a colleague to jump in and change the subject if things start to go sideways. Afterward, debrief with them: "Did you notice what happened? How did it come across to you?" Even just hearing someone else validate your experience can quiet the self-doubt these incidents leave behind.

When dealing with public manipulation, group dynamics matter. Sometimes others will join in, not necessarily because they agree, but because it feels safer than speaking up. Other times, you'll notice silent support from one or two people; find those allies and stick close to them. After the fact, you might hear gossip or be approached by people who want more details about what happened. You don't owe anyone an explanation. A simple script works: "I'm handling the situation directly. Please respect my privacy." This line stops rumors in their tracks and tells people you aren't interested in letting manipulation catch hold.

Suppose group pressure becomes overwhelming, or you feel like there's no way to regain control. In that case, it's okay to leave the event or step away from the group entirely. You never have to stay somewhere you're being publicly targeted or made to feel small. Protecting your peace sometimes means exiting, no apology required.

After public incidents, emotional recovery is just as crucial as any on-the-spot response. Take time alone to process what happened, write about it, talk to your support network, or do something grounding that brings you back to yourself. Remind yourself that public shaming says more about the toxic person than about you. If flying monkeys or third parties who take up the manipulator's cause try to pull you into gossip or pressure you for details, stick to your boundary: "I'm resolving this privately." This steers clear of drama and helps you rebuild your sense of safety.

Public manipulation thrives on silence and confusion. Each time you calmly call out inappropriate behavior or refuse to feed gossip, you chip away at its power. Allies, whether present at the time or supporting you afterward, make a real difference in how quickly you recover and how strong your boundaries remain.

Wrapping up this chapter, remember that difficult conversations aren't just about words; they're about protecting your peace and refusing to be drawn into someone else's drama, especially under the group spotlight. As we move ahead, we'll explore ways to heal and rebuild after these stressful encounters so that your confidence grows stronger with every boundary you set.

Chapter Six

Navigating Family, Parenting, and Shared Obligations

Scripts and Safety Plans for Parallel Parenting with a Toxic Ex

Imagine anxiously checking your phone, dreading your ex's following message about your child's weekend plans. Every text feels loaded, with criticism, sudden schedule demands, or blame. You want what's best for your kids, but you're exhausted by the drama and relentless mind games. When co-parenting becomes a minefield, "let's just be civil for the kids" can feel out of reach. If this sounds familiar, remember, you're not failing; you're handling a challenging situation with strength. That's where parallel parenting comes in.

Parallel parenting works when civil co-parenting isn't possible due to high conflict, manipulation, or volatility. Unlike co-parenting, which requires teamwork, parallel parenting builds boundaries: you both care for your child, but minimize interaction. Think of yourselves as separate managers in the same company; you don't share an office and rarely communicate directly. Contact is kept brief, business-like, and confined to essential child-related matters. Every day, each parent makes independent decisions. At the same time, only major issues (such as health or schooling) are discussed, ideally, always in writing.

Step one is to establish firm communication boundaries. Shift all conversations to email or a parenting app like *OurFamilyWizard* or *TalkingParents*, which time-stamp and archive messages. This helps you ignore provocations and focus solely on information relevant to your child. Never feel obligated to defend or explain; keep everything in writing. If your ex pushes for phone or in-person arguments, use this script: "For clarity, let's keep all parenting communication via email." Repeat as needed, think broken record, not open mic.

During the inevitable drama of accusations and last-minute changes, stick to facts only. On exchange days, use neutral language: "I will be at the designated location at 3:00 p.m. as agreed." If your ex tries to provoke a fight ("You're always late!"), respond, "I am only discussing our child's schedule." For disputes about the court order, reply: "Please refer to the court order for details." These scripts help defuse conflict and keep you focused.

Safety planning is vital when high conflict is involved, especially if emotional outbursts are a risk. Arrange exchanges in public places, school lobbies, police station parking lots, or neutral third-party homes if needed. Some parents enlist trusted friends or relatives for drop-offs to avoid direct contact with their ex. Make sure everyone involved knows and follows the plan.

Documentation is crucial: log every interaction, noting date, time, place, who was present, and any concerning incidents. This isn't just for legal protection; it helps track patterns and preserves details that stress can blur. Use a notebook, app, or shared document if a support person assists you.

Prepare emergency plans. Ensure your child knows alternate emergency contacts (not just parents), and how to ask for help if they feel unsafe. Share these contacts with anyone assisting with exchanges, friends, relatives, or school staff if transfers are on school grounds.

Parallel Parenting Safety & Communication Checklist

- Move all communication to email or a documented app
- Use only neutral language; keep responses brief
- Ignore personal attacks; stick to facts and logistics
- Arrange exchanges at public or third-party locations
- Log every interaction (date, time, details)
- Share emergency contacts with your child and trusted adults
- Have a backup plan for missed exchanges or sudden changes
- Teach your child simple safety steps: who to call, what to say

Parallel parenting isn't a cure-all; it's about minimizing stress and emotional games for you and your children while maintaining their access to both parents. Remember, your efforts to protect your family are meaningful, and resilience can help you navigate these difficulties.

Protecting Your Children from Toxic Relatives

Shielding your kids from toxic relatives is not about locking them in a bubble; it's about helping them grow up with confidence and a sense of safety, even when some family members don't respect boundaries. Toxic relatives, whether they're grandparents, aunts, uncles, or even close family friends, can chip away at a child's self-esteem in subtle ways. Maybe it's the "family joker" who always makes backhanded comments or the grandparent who tries to win affection by guilt-tripping your child with, "If you really loved me, you'd visit more." These moments add up, and kids can internalize messages that leave them anxious or confused about their own value. Recognizing when this is happening and knowing how to talk with your child about it can make a huge difference.

Start by setting clear boundaries with relatives, but also teach your child how to recognize emotional manipulation. Giving your child language and permission to speak up can help you feel more confident and in control of the situation. For example, you might role-play with your child before a family visit. Try saying, "What would you do if Aunt Lisa tells you you're being selfish for not sharing your toy?" Your child could practice replying with, "I like sharing when I'm ready," or, "I don't like that." Another helpful script: "If Grandma says something that makes you feel bad, you can tell her, 'Please don't say that to me.' And you can always come tell me later." Practicing these little scripts builds confidence and helps your child feel prepared.

When explaining toxic behavior or boundaries to children, keep the language age-appropriate and avoid demonizing anyone. Younger kids benefit from simple explanations: "Sometimes people have trouble being kind with their words. If anything makes you feel sad or upset, please tell me." For older kids who notice unfairness or manipulation, say something like, "Everyone makes mistakes, but it's not okay for someone to make you feel guilty or bad about yourself. You're allowed to have your own feelings and choices." These conversations can be awkward at first, but they reassure your child that their feelings matter and encourage honesty in the relationship.

It's important to recognize subtle signs that your child may be affected by toxic relatives. Changes in behavior are often the first clue. Watch for withdrawal after visits, maybe your usually chatty child becomes quiet or seems uneasy. Sudden anxiety around family gatherings, reluctance to visit certain relatives, sleep problems before or after visits, or even physical complaints like headaches or stomachaches can all signal emotional stress. Notice if your child starts parroting negative things said by a relative ("Grandma says I'm too sensitive"), becomes clingy, or suddenly tries hard to please adults at the expense of their own needs. Kids sometimes act out these feelings through irritability, frustration, or even regression, like bedwetting or thumb-sucking in younger children.

When you spot these signs, intervene supportively rather than pouncing on the relative in front of your child. Ask gentle questions: "How did you feel during the visit?" or "Was there anything that made you uncomfortable?" If your child opens up about something hurtful, respond calmly: "Thank you for telling me. That sounds hard. It's okay to feel upset." Avoid dismissing their feelings or rushing to fix things immediately; kids need to know it's safe to talk about uncomfortable moments without fear of making trouble.

Creating a protective network around your child makes all the difference. Connect with teachers, school counselors, coaches, and non-toxic relatives who can keep an eye out for changes in behavior. Send a quick email to trusted adults: "We're working on healthy boundaries at home; please let me know if you notice any changes in [child's name]." This lets others know you're paying attention and builds a team of supportive adults around your child, making it less likely that toxic behavior will go unnoticed or unchecked.

You can also give your family a code word for uncomfortable situations, such as "banana phone" or "purple shoes." If your child says the code word during a visit or call, it means they want to leave or need help without having to explain in front of others. Practice using the code word at home so your child feels comfortable using it in real life.

It's not easy watching your child navigate tricky family dynamics. The urge to shield them entirely is strong, but building resilience through open communication and practical tools is far more powerful. Children who learn how to recognize manipulation and express their feelings early grow up better equipped to set boundaries as adults. The key is staying present and approachable, so your child knows that no matter what happens at grandma's house or anywhere else, they can always come to you for support and understanding.

Managing Sibling Dynamics When a Parent Is Toxic

Growing up under the roof of a toxic parent can twist sibling bonds in ways that follow you well into adulthood. It's more than just the classic "mom always liked you best" squabble. Toxic parents often divide and conquer, using favoritism, scapegoating, and triangulation as their primary tools. Maybe you remember your parent lavishing attention or rewards on one sibling while criticizing or ignoring another. Sometimes, one child is always to blame for family problems, a convenient scapegoat for everything from a sibling's bad grades to a parent's own unhappiness. Over time, this dynamic pits brothers and sisters against each other, leaving some desperate for approval and others convinced they are the family's problem child. Even as adults, you might notice these old patterns creeping in: certain siblings still bend over backward to please the parent, while others keep their distance or carry old wounds that never quite heal.

Trying to talk about the toxic parent with your siblings can feel like navigating a minefield. Some siblings may be enmeshed with the parent, fiercely loyal, or deep in denial about the reality you've lived. Others might echo the parent's narrative, minimizing your experiences or urging you to "let it go." In these moments, it helps to stick to your truth without turning the conversation into a tug-of-war. For example, if your brother dismisses your concerns with, "She's just old-fashioned," you might say, "I respect your experience, but mine is different, and I need to do what's right for me." Keep your words steady and straightforward; don't get pulled into lengthy debates or attempts to prove your pain. If a sibling tries to guilt you for setting boundaries or taking space, you can respond with, "I know we see things differently. I'm making choices that help me feel safe and healthy."

Sometimes, you'll find an ally in the family, another sibling who sees the dysfunction and wants to break the cycle too. If that's the case, protect that connection. Plan sibling-only check-ins where you can talk freely about what's really going on. These conversations are best kept private and separate from group texts or "family meetings," which toxic parents often use to stir up drama or regain control. If a parent insists on having a big sit-down or intervention, set clear limits in advance: "I'm not comfortable discussing my boundaries at a group meeting. I'll talk about my decisions one-on-one if needed." This approach keeps things from becoming a public spectacle or a pile-on.

But what if you're the only one willing to call things out? Or if your siblings side with the parent and shut you out? That heartbreak runs deep, especially when you always imagined your brothers or sisters would be your lifelong teammates. It's common to grieve not just the loss of parental closeness but also the fantasy of sibling unity, the hope that one day everyone would see things clearly or support each other unconditionally. When those bonds are damaged or broken, self-care becomes critical. Let yourself feel sad for what you wish had been different. You might even create your own quiet ritual for letting go: write down your hopes for sibling relationships on slips of paper and burn them safely outside, releasing old expectations into the air.

If journaling helps you process, try this prompt: "What do I need from my siblings, and where else can I find support?" Write honestly about your wishes, maybe it's understanding, backup during tough visits, or just someone to vent to after a rough call with your parent. Then brainstorm where else you can draw strength: close friends, support groups, a partner who listens, or even online communities of people who get it. Sometimes "chosen family" steps up where blood relatives fall short.

It's worth remembering that sibling relationships can shift over time. Sometimes, the brother who once defended the toxic parent grows tired of their games and reaches out years later. Other times, time apart is what keeps the peace. You get to decide how much effort to invest and how close you want to be. Even if your siblings aren't ready or able to meet you halfway right now, it doesn't mean you have to keep living out the same old script. Protecting yourself from family toxicity includes permitting yourself to let go of old roles and finding belonging wherever genuine care exists.

Caring for a Toxic Elder Can Require Balancing Duty and Self-Protection

Few things are as emotionally tangled as caring for a parent or older relative who has always been brutal, manipulative, or even outright cruel. The world tells you, "Family takes care of its own." Culture adds, "Respect your elders." Maybe your community or extended family looks at you sideways if you complain, expecting obedience and gratitude, no matter how toxic the relationship. This pressure can feel suffocating, especially when your reality is far from the usual stories of loving, appreciative elders. I've seen this struggle up close, and it isn't just about managing someone else's needs; it's about carrying years of old pain and guilt while trying to do the right thing.

Take the story of Linda, an only child whose mother criticized her relentlessly for decades. When her mom's health declined, Linda felt the old weight of responsibility crash down. She organized appointments and filled pillboxes, but every visit turned into a verbal minefield: sharp jabs about "never doing enough," guilt over "abandoning" her mother, and reminders of every childhood mistake. Linda lay awake at night, torn between duty and self-preservation, wondering if she was a bad daughter for wanting distance. This tug-of-war is so familiar; love, guilt, resentment, and obligation are all fighting inside you at once.

If you're in this spot, the first step is to define what you can realistically give without losing yourself. Start with a blunt checklist. Write down everything expected of you: driving to appointments, paying bills, grocery shopping, phone calls, and emotional support. Then circle what you can do without serious resentment or damage to your mental health. Draw a hard line under anything that pushes you past your breaking point. Your list might sound like: "I can do weekly groceries and handle the pharmacy run. I cannot be available for daily phone calls or handle emotional meltdowns at midnight." Post this somewhere private as a reminder: you have permission to limit your role.

When asked (or pressured) to do more than you can handle, use short, direct scripts. "I'm not able to do that, but I can help with your groceries on Fridays." You don't have to explain or justify; sometimes, less is more. If relatives chime in with criticism or try to offload extra tasks onto you, reply with "I'm doing what I can within my limits." Stand firm; guilt is their tool, not your truth.

Sometimes, the only way forward is to outsource parts of care or to create more physical and emotional distance. Don't let anyone shame you for needing help; nobody can do this alone, especially when the relationship is already fraught. Explore hiring home care aides, arranging meal deliveries, or exploring assisted living options. Many communities offer senior centers or volunteer visitor programs; these can fill gaps without further draining your energy. Not sure where to start? Try sending an email like, "Hi, I'm looking for resources for elderly care for my parent who lives alone. Do you offer home visits or meal support?" Even small steps toward outside support can bring immense relief.

Emotional boundaries are just as important as practical ones, especially with elders who use manipulation or verbal abuse to keep you off balance. Before every visit or call, take a moment to visualize a mental "shield." Imagine yourself surrounded by a bubble that toxic words can't penetrate. Remind yourself with this affirmation: "I am doing enough, even if it's not appreciated." Use it as armor when old accusations or guilt trips surface. If a conversation turns nasty or crosses your limits, say calmly, "I'm not going to continue this conversation if it gets disrespectful," and then end the call or leave the room if needed.

Suppose you find yourself bracing before every encounter or replaying arguments long after leaving. In that case, that's a sign your boundaries need tightening. Protecting your own emotional health isn't selfish; it's wise and necessary. The old belief that sacrifice equals love doesn't fit here. You're allowed to care without being consumed by it.

Caregiving Limits Checklist

- Tasks I will do (appointments, groceries, bills)

- Tasks I will not do (emotional caretaking, late-night calls)

- My maximum visits per week

- Who else can help (siblings, paid aides)

- Backup plans (senior center support, meal delivery)

Practicing these boundaries takes time and repetition, and yes, probably some backlash from family or the elders themselves. That doesn't mean you're wrong or unloving. It means you're finally putting yourself on the list of people who matter.

How to Explain Boundaries to Partners and "Non-Believers"

Trying to set boundaries with toxic relatives is hard enough on its own. Still, it can get even trickier when your partner or close friends don't get it. Maybe you finally decide to limit visits with a parent who always leaves you feeling wrung out, only to have your partner shrug it off. "You're probably just overreacting," they say, or they roll their eyes when you mention dreading another family dinner. Sometimes, the people you most want on your side don't see the problem, maybe because their own family life was different, or they genuinely think you're making a mountain out of a molehill. This disconnect can make you feel even more isolated, and sometimes it makes you second-guess your decisions.

When you run into skepticism or pushback, clear communication becomes your lifeline. Instead of launching into a rant about everything your relative has ever done wrong (tempting as that might be), ground the conversation in your personal experience. Use "I" statements that focus on how you feel and what you need, not what the other person has failed to see. For example: "I feel emotionally drained after visits with my mother, and I need your support in limiting our time there." Or, "It's important for me to protect our family from unhealthy dynamics, even if they come from people we're supposed to love." These simple statements are less likely to trigger defensiveness and more likely to help your partner see that this isn't about picking fights or holding grudges, it's about protecting your well-being and your household.

Sometimes, though, your partner or friends may minimize what's happening or accidentally sabotage your boundaries. Maybe they encourage more visits or suggest you're being too sensitive. In these moments, remind yourself that you don't have to win them over with endless explanations. Instead, set a boundary around the conversation itself: "I know you see things differently, but I need you to trust my experience." If they try to debate the severity of a family member's behavior, calmly end the discussion: "This isn't up for debate. I'm sharing what I need, not asking for permission." If you feel them encroaching on your decisions, like scheduling a get-together with that difficult relative without asking, be firm: "Please check with me first before making plans involving my family. I need space right now."

Sometimes you'll find that no matter how clearly you explain yourself, some people just can't, or won't, see the toxicity. That's where building a support system outside your immediate circle comes into play. Reaching out to others who have walked this path can be a real game-changer. Consider therapy (either solo or as a couple), where a neutral third party can help unpack family dynamics and validate your feelings. Look for local support groups focused on family estrangement, codependency, or boundaries; many cities host these through community centers or counseling clinics. If leaving home isn't practical, online forums like Reddit's r/raisedbynarcissists or Facebook groups devoted to family boundaries offer nonjudgmental spaces full of people who "get it." For those who prefer more privacy, various therapist directories like *Psychology Today* or *TherapyDen* let you search for professionals specializing in toxic family issues.

Finding validation outside your immediate circle doesn't mean giving up on your partner's support forever; it just gives you breathing room and perspective while you work through tough spots at home. It's perfectly okay to say, "I'd love for us to talk about this in counseling," or "I'm working on this with my group and just need your patience right now." Over time, many partners come around when they see the positive impact boundaries have on your mood and stress levels.

If you're feeling isolated or misunderstood as you work through these changes, remember that countless others are wrestling with the same tensions, struggling to balance loyalty, self-respect, and old expectations. Surround yourself with people who encourage growth rather than guilt, whether they're friends, professionals, or virtual allies. You don't have to justify healthy change to everyone; sometimes the only permission you need is your own.

As we wrap up this chapter on family and shared obligations, keep in mind that healthy boundaries aren't just about who you keep at arm's length; they're also about who gets close enough to help you thrive. The next chapter will shift focus from survival to healing and rebuilding your confidence in every relationship that matters most.

Chapter Seven

Protecting Yourself Professionally from Toxicity at Work

Spotting the Toxic Boss Includes Behaviors You Can't Ignore

Picture this: you're working quietly when your boss publicly points out your past mistake, using sarcasm that leaves you embarrassed in front of everyone. Repeated incidents can make you feel vulnerable and unsure of your security at work. Recognizing this impact helps you feel understood and motivated to seek support.

Not all tough managers are toxic. There's a key difference between high standards and harmful behavior. Supportive leaders set clear expectations, offer constructive feedback, and acknowledge your efforts, no matter how small. Toxic bosses, instead, keep you guessing whether you'll receive praise or humiliation. One day, you get thanks for extra hours; the next, your mistake "sets everyone back." This inconsistency is itself harmful.

So what makes a boss truly toxic? It's about persistent patterns, not one-off lapses. The first major red flag is consistent public humiliation. If your boss singles you out for criticism in meetings, makes jokes at your expense, or uses sarcasm to shut down your ideas, pay attention. Recognizing these signs helps you identify toxic behaviors early and take appropriate action. This is not feedback; it's a way to dominate. Another sign is taking credit for your work; if, time after time, your ideas show up in your boss's presentations without acknowledgment, it's not a fluke but a deliberate act.

Toxic bosses also undermine employees, changing deadlines or expectations without warning, withholding resources, or excluding you from key discussions, only to blame you for missing information. The shifting ground keeps you off balance and fearful; this is not "fast-paced leadership" but sabotage.

Checklist of Toxic Boss Behaviors

- Regular public criticism or mockery

- Taking credit for your work or ideas

- Setting unachievable tasks, then blaming you for failing

- Changing rules or expectations without notice

- Excluding people from essential meetings or updates

- Giving only vague directions, but harsh consequences

To clarify the line between harsh and toxic, consider performance reviews. A demanding leader gives clear, actionable feedback, highlights areas for growth, and collaborates on next steps. You leave knowing where you stand. A toxic boss lists only your mistakes in detail, questions your competence in front of others, and never acknowledges what you've done right. Or they dangle raises and promotions, promising to "revisit next quarter" but never following through.

Working for someone like this affects more than your confidence. Toxic bosses heighten stress and cause burnout, leaving you feeling overwhelmed and helpless. Developing coping strategies, such as mindfulness or seeking peer support, can help you manage emotional responses. Understanding this link can inspire you to take steps to protect your mental health and seek positive change.

Am I Experiencing Toxic Management?

Ask yourself:

- Do you feel anxious before boss meetings?
- Are you blamed for things outside your control?
- Does your boss mock your concerns publicly?
- Do promises about advancement quietly disappear?
- Are you excluded from vital communications?
- Do rules change without any notice?

Suppose you answer "yes" to several of them. In that case, this likely isn't just a demanding boss; it's a toxic environment affecting your mental health and job satisfaction.

Try Journaling

Each day this week, note any workplace interactions that left you uneasy or undervalued. Record details like the date, time, location, and whether incidents occurred publicly or privately, including who was involved. Documenting specific behaviors helps you build a clear record, empowering you to recognize patterns and take informed action.

Recognizing these toxic patterns is the first step in reclaiming confidence at work. When you identify behaviors like public humiliation or credit theft, consider how to communicate your concerns professionally. Approaching HR or a trusted manager with documented examples can help you seek support and initiate change, protecting your well-being and professional growth.

Scripts for Handling Manipulative Coworkers in Meetings

Meetings can quickly become a battleground when you've got a manipulative coworker in the mix. You might recognize the signs: someone waits until you finish explaining an idea and then rephrases it as if it's their own, winning nods from the boss. Another favorite move is the backhanded compliment, like, "That's a creative suggestion, much better than last time!" Sometimes, it's just those "jokes" about your past mistakes, slipped in front of managers, that hang in the air longer than they should. These tactics aren't just annoying; over time, they chip away at your credibility and confidence. If you've ever left a meeting questioning whether you overreacted or wishing you'd spoken up, you're not alone.

Handling this nonsense requires both quick thinking and a calm presence. When a coworker tries to claim your idea, don't get flustered or defensive. Instead, use a script that politely but firmly puts your name back in the mix. Try something like, 'Thanks for building on my idea, Sam. I want to add...' This approach acknowledges their contribution without letting them erase yours. If they push further or try to dominate the discussion, keep your tone neutral and repeat your point. If you notice a pattern over several meetings, start mentioning your ideas early in the agenda or in email follow-ups so there's a record. Document these incidents to feel more confident and in control of your responses.

Public put-downs and "jokes" are another level of subtle sabotage. Someone might say, "Remember when you mixed up those numbers last quarter? Classic!" Everyone laughs, except you. Rather than laugh along or shrink away, redirect with a calm, assertive statement: "Let's keep feedback constructive and focused on today's work." This not only addresses the behavior but signals to everyone else that you expect a professional environment. If they try to make it seem like you're too sensitive, don't take the bait. Just stay steady and move the conversation forward: "I'd like to get back to the main topic. Can we come back to the agenda?"

Body language is your secret weapon here. Sit tall, shoulders back, feet planted. Maintain eye contact with whoever's speaking, even if they're being difficult. Keep your hands relaxed on the table. Avoid crossing your arms or fidgeting, which can signal discomfort or frustration. Your voice should stay measured and precise; no need to shout or rush. When you speak, pause for a beat at the start and end of your point; this signals authority and helps others tune in. If someone interrupts, lift your hand slightly (as if you're signaling "wait") and say, "I'd like to finish my thought." Practicing this kind of presence outside meetings, in front of a mirror or with a trusted friend, boosts your comfort level when things get tense.

Gaining allies is often overlooked but can be a game-changer if there's someone on the team who seems fair-minded or supportive. Connect with them before meetings. Share your concerns without gossiping, something like, "I noticed my ideas sometimes get lost in the shuffle during meetings. Would you be open to backing me up if it happens again?" During meetings, allies can reinforce your contributions by saying, "That builds on what you just said," or simply nodding in support.

Group dynamics can get tricky if one person dominates or stirs up drama. If a colleague keeps steering conversations off-track or sabotaging ideas, redirect politely but firmly: "We're veering off subject, let's bring it back to our main points." Or suggest tabling side discussions for later: "Can we discuss that offline? I want to make sure we stay on schedule." These phrases help keep meetings focused while signaling that distractions won't derail you.

After a meeting where tensions run high or manipulative tactics were used, make it a habit to jot down what happened while it's fresh, who said what, how others responded, and any key phrases used. Note-taking isn't about keeping a secret diary; it's about creating an objective record if issues escalate later. Save any relevant emails as well. Suppose things get worse or you need to escalate the problem to HR or management down the line. In that case, you'll have clear evidence of patterns rather than vague memories.

An Assertive Meeting Presence Checklist

- Sit with good posture and maintain steady eye contact.

- Use calm, controlled hand gestures.

- Speak in short sentences; pause before and after key points.

- If interrupted, gently raise your hand and repeat, "I'd like to finish my thought."

- Redirect negative comments: "Let's keep things constructive."

- Document key exchanges right after meetings while details are fresh.

Navigating manipulative coworkers isn't about winning every exchange; it's about protecting your voice and reputation without being drawn into unnecessary drama or conflict. With practice and these scripts in hand, you'll find it gets easier to hold your ground and steer meetings toward respect and productivity.

Protecting Your Reputation from Gossip and Smear Campaigns

It starts quietly, someone whispers in the break room, "Did you hear what Jamie said in the meeting?" or you notice side glances when you walk by. Toxic coworkers often use gossip and subtle rumor-spreading to cast doubt on your skills, intentions, or even your character. Sometimes it's a string of offhand comments about your "lack of commitment" when you leave on time, or questions about your loyalty if you push back on a questionable project. These tactics aren't just annoying; they're corrosive. Whisper campaigns can chip away at your reputation before you even realize what's happening. The real danger is underestimating them. You might think, "It's just office talk, it'll blow over," but rumors, mainly when repeated and left unchallenged, can stick. Over time, they may influence how others view your competence, reliability, or even trustworthiness. The result? Projects dry up, promotions go to others, and your confidence takes a hit.

The best defense is to take control of your own narrative before someone else does it for you. When you hear hints that your name is being dragged through the mud, it's tempting to ignore it or get defensive, but there's a more innovative way. Start by regularly sharing positive updates with your supervisors and stakeholders. Did you solve a tricky problem or get good feedback from a client? Bring it up casually in emails, team meetings, or one-on-ones, not as bragging, but as transparency. That way, if someone tries to question your contributions, those above you already have context for your value. Another move is to build cross-department relationships. If your reputation only depends on one group, it's easier for rumors to spread unchecked. But if folks from other teams know you as approachable and competent, it's much harder for a smear campaign to take root.

Addressing gossip directly can feel awkward, but letting it go only allows it to fester. If you hear comments about yourself or see conversations turning sour, consider stepping in with calm confidence. You might say, "I prefer not to discuss coworkers who aren't present," which puts the brakes on gossip without escalating conflict. If you're being pressured to comment on office drama or defend yourself against vague accusations, redirect: "Let's focus on the project at hand." Keep your tone friendly but unwavering; don't offer excuses or explanations where none are needed. These phrases set a clear boundary and signal that you're not interested in playing the rumor game.

Sometimes the situation calls for more than just redirecting conversations. Notice a pattern of negative talk that's starting to affect your opportunities or standing at work. It may be time to take a more formal approach. Start by documenting what's happening. Keep a private log with dates, times, and specifics, who said what, where it happened, and who else was present. Emails, messages, or casual notes after meetings can all be helpful. Ask for written references or positive feedback from supervisors or colleagues who respect your work. This isn't about stockpiling ammunition but creating a clear record in case things escalate.

When the smear campaign crosses into territory that threatens your job security or mental well-being, consider talking to management or HR. Go in prepared, with your documentation organized by incidents and dates. Share facts rather than feelings: "On March 3rd, I learned that my coworker told others I missed a deadline I had actually completed early. Here's the email thread confirming my delivery." Presenting a timeline helps HR see the behavior as a pattern rather than isolated drama. If you have allies who can vouch for your professionalism or have witnessed incidents firsthand, ask if they'd be willing to put their observations in writing or speak up if needed.

Your Reputation Management Action Plan

Let's take a few minutes to investigate:

- Where does most gossip originate in your workplace?

- Who tends to get caught up in it?

Make a list of positive facts about your recent work, big wins, helpful actions, and specific feedback, and consider how you can weave them naturally into conversations or updates this week.

Keep in mind that standing up to toxic gossip doesn't mean getting tangled in every rumor or fighting every fire. Sometimes the most powerful thing you can do is remain steady and focused on your work while quietly making sure those who matter see the real story. Over time, consistent professionalism and positive visibility will outlast any whisper campaign, plus, you'll protect not just your reputation but your sense of self-worth at work.

Documenting Toxic Behavior With Paper Trails and HR Strategies

Relying on intuition won't protect you in a toxic work environment; documentation will. Written records are your protection when things get difficult, shifting a situation from "he said, she said" to actual, actionable evidence. Think of your documentation as a living archive: track dates, times, people present, and direct quotes. This isn't paranoia; it's safeguarding your reputation and future.

Start with the basics:

- Record the date, time, and location of every concerning incident.

- Write out exactly what was said using direct quotes, list witnesses, and describe outcomes (did you walk away, did the tone shift, did someone else react?).

- Be precise and objective, no embellishments or opinions. The more factual your notes, the more useful they'll be if you ever need them.

Use a small notebook or a private document on your personal device (never a work device or company cloud account). If digital, store files in secure, private apps or encrypted cloud storage, like Google Drive or Dropbox, using your personal email. Give files neutral names so they don't attract attention. Keep paper records away from the workplace, in your bag or car, not your desk. Back up digital records in at least two locations, so you're not left empty-handed if you leave your job abruptly.

A simple incident log template:

- Date/Time:

- Location:

- People Present:

- What Happened (word-for-word):

- Immediate Outcome:

- Follow-Up (if any):

Spreadsheets work well for digital logs, allowing you to sort by person or incident type. Always use strong passwords and two-factor authentication. Never email documentation to your work address; always use personal accounts.

When problematic patterns emerge, such as repeated comments, exclusion, or unfair blame, consider escalating. Before contacting HR, review your documentation and select clear examples that show a pattern, not isolated mistakes. HR is more likely to respond to concise, factual information.

Write a brief and neutral email, such as:

Hi [HR Contact],

I want to report several recurring incidents that are affecting my ability to do my job. Here's a summary:

On March 5th at 10:00 AM in the conference room, [Name] told me, "You're clearly not cut out for this role," in front of three staff (see attached log).

On March 12th, [Name] emailed me, accusing me of missing a deadline I had met (see attached email).

I have more documentation if needed and am seeking support to address this.

Thanks for your help,

[Your Name]

Attach minimal documentation first; keep other records for later if needed.

After emailing HR, follow up if you don't hear back within a day or two: "Just confirming you received my previous email regarding workplace incidents." Store all HR-related correspondence in a dedicated folder on your personal device, noting when you sent each message and when you received replies.

Keep documenting after you report to HR. Monitor for changes in behavior; sometimes the situation improves, sometimes subtle retaliation begins. Record dates and details for anything that occurs after the report. This ongoing log can be crucial if someone later claims your report caused problems that weren't there.

Incident Documentation Checklist

- Log each incident with date, time, location, and direct quotes.

- Note every witness.

- Store documentation only on personal devices or in cloud services with strong   passwords.

- Use neutral file/folder names.

- Back up digital files in more than one place.

- Write concise, factual HR summaries.

- Follow up with HR for confirmation.

- Continue tracking all relevant interactions after reporting.

Documenting toxic behavior isn't paranoid, it's smart. Detailed records can help you advocate for yourself and provide solid proof if your professionalism is questioned. Most importantly, keeping thorough records can offer peace of mind and remind you that you're not alone.

What to Do If You're Targeted After Speaking Up (Retaliation)

Sometimes the fallout from standing up to toxic behavior at work hits you in ways you never expected. You go to HR, lay out your concerns, and then, suddenly, things change. Your calendar fills up with meetings you're not invited to. Projects you once led move quietly to someone else's plate. Emails skip your inbox, and suddenly, performance reviews include vague criticisms you've never heard before. It's not always loud or obvious, but the message is clear: you're being pushed to the sidelines for daring to speak up.

Retaliation can sneak in under the radar. Maybe your boss or coworker stops responding to your questions. You find yourself left out of meaningful discussions, or you notice a pile-up of new duties not matched to your skills, almost as if someone hopes you'll trip up. Sometimes you get called out for "not being a team player" or for minor mistakes that were overlooked before. It's easy to second-guess yourself or wonder if you're imagining it, but if this pattern starts after you report toxicity, don't brush it off.

The first thing you need is awareness. Start by updating your documentation right away, record every change in your workload, every new expectation, and every time you're excluded from vital meetings or communications. Don't just track the big stuff; even minor snubs or new tasks matter because patterns speak volumes. If your job description changes or you're assigned tasks outside your usual scope, note it down with dates and details. Save emails or memos that reference your performance or responsibilities, and keep these records off company devices whenever possible.

You don't have to go through this alone. Reach out to trusted coworkers who've witnessed changes since your report was filed. Sometimes, having an ally who can confirm what's happening makes all the difference. If your workplace has an employee assistance program (EAP), now's the time to use it. These programs offer confidential guidance and can connect you with outside resources. If you're unionized, contact your representative immediately; they can help document retaliation and stand with you in meetings. For those without a union or EAP, legal hotlines (often run by state labor boards or nonprofit organizations) can offer advice about next steps and clarify your rights.

When it's time to address retaliation directly, stay calm and professional. Go to HR or a higher manager with clear documentation and a neutral tone. You might say, "Since my report, I've noticed the following changes..." then list specific examples, dates, meetings missed, new duties assigned, and any feedback that feels out of character for your history at the company. Ask for clarification: "Can we clarify expectations moving forward?" This puts the ball in their court and signals that you're attentive but not emotional or confrontational. If they dodge the topic or seem vague, ask for written confirmation of what's expected of you now. Keep every response for your records.

It's normal for this process to take a toll on your mental well-being. Stress can creep up, such as sleepless nights, headaches, or constant worry about what might happen next. Don't isolate yourself. Find a therapist or counselor familiar with workplace trauma; they'll help you process what's happening and build coping strategies so stress doesn't swallow your life outside of work. Even if talking to someone feels awkward at first, it usually pays off.

Building a small support network is crucial. Whether it's a friend who listens without judgment, a family member who keeps an eye out for signs of burnout, or an online group where people share similar stories, you need safe spaces where you aren't doubted or blamed. Sometimes just knowing someone else has survived this makes all the difference.

If things worsen or HR fails to act meaningfully, it might be time to plan an exit strategy. Jot down what matters most: financial needs, references secured, and what kind of workplace culture you want next time. Scrub your resume, start low-key networking, and look for opportunities without drawing attention at work. A checklist can help: Are all personal files backed up? Do you have copies of positive reviews? Have you lined up emergency contacts? If legal action becomes necessary, consult with an employment lawyer before resigning; they'll advise on timing and documentation.

Experiencing retaliation after speaking up isn't just unfair, it's a signal that your workplace values silence over safety. As tough as it feels in the moment, remember that protecting your own peace and dignity matters more than any single job title. Stress from toxic environments can follow you home if left unchecked; taking steps now can prevent deeper wounds later.

In wrapping up this chapter, remember: work should never make you feel powerless or alone for doing the right thing. If you find yourself targeted for speaking up, use every tool at your disposal, including documentation, allies, and professional support, to reclaim control over your career and well-being. The next chapter shifts focus from survival mode at work to healing and rebuilding self-worth in all areas of life, because you deserve so much more than just getting by.

Chapter Eight

Healing, Recovery, and Rebuilding Self-Worth

Unlearning Self-Blame and Shame

You find yourself staring in the bathroom mirror after a tough day, replaying a conversation where you apologized for something that wasn't your fault. Those words echo: "Maybe I'm just too much," or "Why can't I get this right?" You feel exposed and small, believing every flaw is visible. This is how shame and self-blame linger after toxic relationships. They settle deep, making you question your worthiness of kindness or respect. Carrying that weight is exhausting. You may have found yourself thinking it's all your fault, that if you were better, things would be different. Remember, you are deserving of kindness and understanding, and healing begins with feeling safe to explore these feelings.

Shame is especially insidious. It doesn't help us grow; it convinces us we're broken or unlovable. Over time, shame saps your motivation to try new things or ask for support. You might steer clear of opportunities because you secretly believe you'll fail or that others are burdened by your "problems." Self-blame fills the space shame creates, trapping you in endless reruns of what you "should have done differently." The truth?

Neither shame nor self-blame is genuinely yours. They're handed over by people unable to accept responsibility for their actions.

"Whose Voice Is This?" Letting Go of Toxic Messages

Take a moment to jot down the harsh statements you say to yourself when you mess up or feel anxious: things like, "You're so sensitive," "You always mess things up," or "No one could really love you." After writing each one, ask yourself: Whose voice is this? Did it start with a critical parent, a dismissive partner, or a belittling boss? Label each message with that source, even if you're not certain. This helps you see that these judgments are echoes from others, not truths about you.

Next, bring to mind your younger self, someone deserving of support, who maybe didn't always receive it. Write a letter to the younger you. Offer forgiveness for carrying blame that was never yours. Be reassuring, write "You did the best you could," or "You weren't responsible for another's anger." If you like, keep the letter private or read it aloud when shame resurfaces. Honesty matters more than perfection here.

Toxic beliefs like "I'm too sensitive," "It's my fault," or "I never get things right" stick around due to years of manipulation. Challenge these beliefs with self-compassion by rewriting them. Change "I'm too sensitive" to "My feelings matter." Replace "It's my fault" with "I am not responsible for others' choices." Instead of "I never get things right," say "Mistakes are part of growth." Replacing these thoughts can help you feel more empowered and in control of your healing journey. Repeat your new, kinder statements to reinforce your worth.

Try to Visualize

Visualization can help reduce the hold shame has. Close your eyes and imagine the shame or blame you carry as heavy stones in a box. Pick up each stone, name whose message it really is, and place it in the box. Once the box is filled, picture handing it back to its owner or leaving it where it can't burden you anymore. Notice how much lighter you feel as you move away and breathe deeply. This exercise can help you feel hopeful about releasing what no longer serves you, opening space for healing and growth.

Try Meditation

To try a meditative approach, sit comfortably and close your eyes. Imagine a gentle light at your heart spreading warmth. With each breath out, picture releasing the guilt and heaviness that never belonged to you. With each breath in, remind yourself: "I am enough as I am." If blame returns, imagine those thoughts passing by like clouds, not something you need to hold onto.

You are not defined by others' criticism, disappointment, or anger. Unlearning shame means recognizing what is not yours and, maybe for the first time, choosing to speak with the compassion and care you always needed. These steps don't deny what happened; they allow you to finally let go of burdens that were never meant for you.

Journaling Prompts for Reclaiming Self-Esteem

After living through a toxic relationship, you might feel like your sense of self is in pieces. The person you used to be, confident, funny, resilient, can seem far away. One of the most effective ways to start finding your way back is through intentional journaling. This isn't about keeping a diary of complaints or chores. It's about putting your thoughts and feelings somewhere safe and private, then using that space to rebuild who you are gently. Research shows that expressive writing can help untangle emotional knots, lower anxiety, and boost healing after difficult experiences. When you write about what happened, how you felt, and what you want for yourself, your brain begins to process pain in a new way. It's as if the chaos in your head starts to line up on the page. You get distance from old stories and make room for new ones.

Journaling is more than venting; done with intention, it becomes a tool for reclaiming self-worth and rediscovering your identity. Start with prompts designed to bring your strengths and values into focus. Think about a time you overcame something challenging. Maybe you moved to a new city alone, raised kids through uncertainty, or got back up after heartbreak. Ask yourself: what strengths did I use? Was it courage, patience, humor, or resourcefulness? Write about that moment in detail. Next, list five qualities you genuinely admire about yourself, especially those others tried to shut down. Maybe you're deeply empathetic or fiercely protective. Perhaps you refuse to give up on your dreams. Even if someone once called these traits "too much," write them down as badges of honor.

Go deeper by exploring what makes you feel most at home in your own skin. What activities, places, or routines help you feel like the truest version of yourself? Is it reading by a sunny window, hiking through the woods, painting late at night, or laughing with friends who get you? Write about why these moments matter and how you can invite more of them into your life. Recognizing these activities supports your journey of self-compassion and healing from toxic relationships.

Another powerful practice is keeping an "evidence journal" or "self-esteem file." This is a running log, digital or physical, where you collect real proof of your worth. Save screenshots of kind messages, jot down compliments you receive (even small ones), and note every personal win. Did you stand up for yourself at work? Did a friend thank you for being there? Did you finish a task even when anxiety tried to stop you? Record it all. On bad days, flip through this file as a reminder that progress is real and setbacks are not the end of your story.

If traditional journaling feels stiff or forced, try creative approaches that fit your style. Some people love mind-mapping, a way to visualize their support system or hopes with circles and lines rather than sentences. Start with your name at the center, then branch out to people, places, and activities that give you hope or joy. Notice where the branches feel strong and where they seem thin; this can help you see what needs more attention in your life. Others turn to doodling or collage, especially when words get stuck. Grab old magazines or scraps of paper and make a visual board of dreams for the future, no rules, just intuition guiding what feels right.

You might also pick one prompt per week as a gentle ritual: "Describe a time I felt proud of myself," "Write about someone who made a difference in my life," or "What would I tell a close friend going through what I've survived?" The goal isn't perfection; it's honesty and exploration. Some days your writing will flow, other days it may be a struggle, but every entry counts as proof that you're showing up for yourself.

If staying consistent is tough, set up small rewards for filling a page or completing an exercise, a favorite snack, a walk outside, or listening to music that lifts your spirits. You can even use voice notes on your phone if handwriting feels like too much some days. The point is to keep finding ways back to yourself, piece by piece.

Journaling isn't just an emotional dumping ground; over time, it becomes a record of survival and growth. As the pages fill up, patterns emerge, you see what drains you, what lifts you, and what parts of yourself are returning stronger than ever. This written proof is private empowerment: when doubt creeps in, you have tangible reminders of the real progress happening inside and out.

Mindfulness and Grounding Practices for Emotional Recovery

When life with a toxic person has left your nervous system feeling fried, even simple moments can trigger anxiety. Your heart races, your thoughts speed up, and suddenly you're back in that old emotional storm. Mindfulness is like an anchor in those waters; it's the skill of bringing your attention to the present with kindness and curiosity, rather than letting your mind get swept away by old fears or painful memories. After toxic stress, your body can stay stuck in "fight or flight" mode long after the danger has passed. Mindfulness helps reset that alarm system, lowering stress hormones and quieting the inner critic that loves to replay every mistake. Studies show that regularly practicing mindfulness not only calms anxiety but can actually shrink the part of your brain responsible for panic and emotional hijacking, while strengthening areas linked to self-control and compassion. This isn't just feel-good talk; it's science-backed and accessible to everyone.

There's a common myth that mindfulness means sitting still and emptying your mind for an hour. That's not true. Mindfulness can be as quick as three minutes and as simple as noticing your breath or the feeling of your feet on the ground. When you catch yourself spiraling, maybe reliving an argument or imagining worst-case scenarios, you can use grounding techniques to pull your focus back from the past or future into what's happening right now. One of my favorites is the 5-4-3-2-1 sensory awareness practice. Pause and name five things you can see around you, four things you can touch, three sounds you hear, two things you can smell, and one thing you can taste. If you're in a hurry or overwhelmed, try this shortcut: name three things you see, two you hear, and one physical sensation (like the chair under you or your hand on your heart). These small acts send a message to your body that you are safe in this moment.

If you're new to mindfulness or have trauma in your history, it's essential to go slow and listen to your body. For some people, closing their eyes or sitting still feels uncomfortable or even unsafe. That's okay, mindfulness isn't about forcing yourself to relax. Instead, choose what works for you. Try mindful movement, like walking slowly and noticing how each step feels underfoot, or do gentle stretches while focusing on the sensations in your muscles. Even washing dishes or brushing your teeth can be mindful if you really pay attention to the sights, sounds, and sensations of the task.

For those who like structure, here's a simple three-minute body scan you can try anytime: Sit or lie down comfortably. Breathe in through your nose and out through your mouth. Bring your attention to the top of your head. Notice any sensations, tingling, warmth, or coolness. Spend a moment there, then shift focus to your forehead, eyes, cheeks, and jaw, relaxing each area if possible, but not judging if tension stays. Move down through your neck, shoulders, arms, chest, belly, hips, legs, and feet, pausing briefly at each spot. If thoughts pop up (and they will), notice them and gently bring your focus back to your body. After about 3 minutes, see how you feel now compared to when you started.

If sitting quietly is tough, your mind races, or you get restless, try guided practices using free mindfulness apps like *Insight Timer* or *Calm*. Search for "body scan," "grounding," or "anxiety relief." Many of these apps let you choose the voice, length, and mood that best fit you. If audio feels too much at first, just set a timer and focus on slow breathing: inhale for four counts, hold for two, exhale for six. If your thoughts start sprinting off into worries or flashbacks, bring your attention back to the physical sensation of air moving in and out of your nose.

Sometimes skepticism creeps in. You might think, "This is too simple," or, "I'm just not a meditation person." That's normal, plenty of people feel awkward at first or worry they aren't "doing it right." The trick is consistency over perfection. A few minutes most days rewires your stress response far more than one perfect session a week. And if sitting still doesn't work for you right now? Walk slowly around the block with all five senses engaged, stretch while naming each muscle group aloud, or even hum quietly to yourself as you focus on the vibration in your chest.

The point isn't to erase all stress or have mystical experiences; it's to build a toolkit for calming yourself when emotions threaten to take over. Whether you use breathwork in the car before work, the 5-4-3-2-1 exercise during a tense phone call, or guided audio before bed, each act of mindfulness is a step toward reclaiming peace from chaos.

Find Your "Chosen Family" to Build a Resilient Support System

There's a unique comfort in being surrounded by people who get you, even if you don't share DNA or family history. That's the beauty of "chosen family." This isn't just a buzzword; it's a lifeline, mainly after you've survived the emotional chaos of toxic relationships. Chosen family means hand-picking those who respect your boundaries, celebrate your wins, and offer genuine support. Unlike biological relatives, these are people you actively want in your life because they show up with kindness and honesty, not obligation or guilt. For many, especially those who never felt truly safe or valued at home, chosen family is a second chance at belonging.

Biological families can be nurturing, but for some, they're the source of deep wounds. Maybe your relatives are always critical or never listen; maybe it's more subtle, like feeling invisible at every gathering. Chosen family flips that script. Here, support isn't transactional. There's no scoreboard keeping track of favors owed. Instead, you're building relationships based on mutual care and respect. You can show up as yourself, messy edges and all, without fear of being shamed or dismissed.

Take a careful look at your current circle. Who energizes you? Who leaves you feeling drained? Grab a piece of paper and sketch out your connections, a "relationship map." Put yourself at the center, then draw lines to friends, coworkers, neighbors, or family members. Next to each name, jot down how you feel after spending time with them: lighter, heavier, supported, anxious, or neutral. This isn't about judging anyone; it's about getting honest with yourself about who brings comfort and who brings chaos. You might spot gaps, maybe there aren't enough people you trust with your real feelings, or perhaps you're clinging to connections out of habit or guilt rather than true closeness.

Finding new, supportive people doesn't mean you have to overhaul your social life overnight. Start small and stay open-minded. One solid way to meet like-minded folks is to join groups with shared interests, such as book clubs, fitness classes, art workshops, faith communities, or volunteer activities. If in-person options feel daunting or aren't accessible, online spaces can be rich sources of connection too. Many communities have Facebook groups for local events, hobby-based forums, or apps designed to help people make new friends. Support groups (both virtual and in-person) are beneficial if you're looking for others who understand what it means to heal from toxic relationships. You can find these through local counseling centers, libraries, or organizations focused on mental health and recovery. If you're nervous about attending alone, ask if you can bring a friend or even attend the first meeting virtually.

Let's say you join a community garden or a weekly crafting night. Show up regularly, even if you feel awkward at first; consistency builds trust over time. Start with small talk if deep conversation feels intimidating; sometimes friendships grow from shared laughter over spilled paint or burnt cookies. As comfort develops, try sharing a little more of yourself: "I'm working on being more open, here's what I need in a friend: honesty and kindness." Or if you sense someone is trustworthy but aren't sure how to move forward, try: "I value genuine connection, and I'm looking for friends who support each other."

It's wise to watch for red flags and green flags as these new connections grow. Red flags include people who ignore your boundaries, gossip about others in your presence, constantly play the victim, or only reach out when they need something. If someone makes fun of your feelings, pressures you into things that feel wrong, or drains your energy every time you talk, take note; it might be time to step back. On the flip side, green flags often signal respect for your time and opinions, consistency in words and actions, a willingness to apologize when wrong, and an ability to celebrate your successes without jealousy.

Here's a quick checklist to help spot supportive friends:

- Do they listen without interrupting?

- Respect your limits?

- Encourage your growth?

- Apologize when they mess up?

- Cheer for you without competition?

These are signs of healthy relationships worth nurturing. Don't be afraid to talk openly about boundaries as things deepen; try saying, "I'm working on keeping my life drama-free. I appreciate friends who communicate directly." If someone is truly supportive, they'll understand and respect these needs.

Building chosen family isn't about finding perfect people; it's about finding people who make you feel safe enough to be imperfect. Over time, these relationships become the roots that keep you grounded and the wings that help you soar. Finding them takes patience and courage, but every step toward authentic connection is a step away from isolation.

Restoring Trust in Yourself and Others After Betrayal

Betrayal shatters not only your faith in others but also your trust in yourself. Repeated lies, manipulation, or broken promises can leave you questioning your instincts: "How did I not see that coming?" or, "Why didn't I trust my gut?" Over time, such experiences erode confidence, making even simple decisions feel daunting and loaded with anxiety. The ease and safety you once felt in your judgment may feel out of reach.

Rebuilding self-trust takes time and small, deliberate steps. Start with micro-decisions, tiny, everyday choices. Each morning, choose what you want for breakfast based on your own preference, not what you "should" eat. Notice how these choices make you feel. Keep a journal tracking these decisions and their outcomes; for example, "Took a walk after work instead of scrolling my phone, felt calmer." Following through on even small promises to yourself signals that your word matters, helping to rebuild trust slowly.

Celebrate when you honor your commitments, no matter how minor they are. If you call a friend as planned or take a well-needed break, give yourself credit. Recognizing these moments, even small ones, will help rebuild confidence. When doubts creep in, look back at your journal for evidence that you make good decisions for yourself.

Restoring trust in others after betrayal is another challenge. It can be tempting to either trust too quickly or withdraw completely, but balance is key. Move slowly, pay attention to whether people's actions match their words, and maintain your boundaries. Don't ignore red flags out of loneliness, and don't turn away from genuine connections out of fear. Consider whether someone keeps promises, is honest even when it's hard, respects your boundaries, and takes responsibility when wrong. If the answers are mostly yes, the relationship has potential.

Communicate openly about your needs and boundaries. You might say, "I value honesty and reliability, let's work on building trust together." You're not seeking perfection, just consistency and openness. Pay attention to the other person's behavior over time, not just their words. Absolute trust grows in the small moments: showing up when promised, listening without judgment, and respecting privacy.

Forgiveness is often misunderstood. It doesn't mean excusing harmful behavior; it's about freeing yourself from resentment and refusing to let the betrayer control your emotions or future actions. If you're ready, try a forgiveness meditation by imagining the person at a distance and saying, "I release the hold you have on my life," or write a letter expressing your feelings, not to send, but to let go of the burden.

Reflect on what trust means to you now. Ask yourself: "How would I like to experience trust moving forward?" Maybe it's giving others a bit of grace before fully opening up, or being patient with yourself as you learn to listen to your instincts again. Healing takes time; there's no preset deadline. It's an ongoing practice of honesty with yourself and cautious openness with others.

Restoring trust requires patience and attention, but it is possible after betrayal. The more you consistently show up for yourself, the more your inner compass will reset. With renewed self-trust, you'll find it easier to build healthy, confident connections.

Some days, healing will feel like a battle; others, as simple as a single honest choice or kind gesture. This chapter has focused on reclaiming what toxic people may have damaged: your self-faith and your ability to form safe, genuine relationships. In the next chapter, the focus shifts from survival to thriving, creating joy, purpose, and fulfillment in every area of your life.

Chapter Nine

Prevention and Pattern-Breaking for the Future

Creating Your Personal Red Flag Checklist

You're sitting in a crowded restaurant, laughter and music all around. Still, you notice your new friend glancing at your phone whenever it buzzes. Their comments about your other friends are sharp. You brush it off, maybe it's just nerves, you think. But that uneasy feeling lingers. Recognizing these subtle warnings can boost your confidence in trusting your gut, making your red-flag checklist your best ally.

Everyone's experience with toxic relationships looks a little different, so there's no one-size-fits-all list. You might have a boss who regularly takes credit for your work, a partner who jokes about your insecurities, or a friend who only calls when they need something. What matters is learning to spot the patterns that have tripped you up before. Start by thinking back on times you ignored your instincts and later regretted it.

- What were the early signs?

- Did you notice jealousy disguised as concern?

- Subtle digs hidden in sarcasm?

- Promises that kept getting broken?

Write down these moments, even the ones that seemed small at the time. This process isn't about blaming yourself; it's about empowering yourself with a clear, updated red flag checklist so you feel more in control moving forward.

Your Top 10 Red Flags

Take a few minutes for this exercise. On a piece of paper or in your notes app, jot down your "Top 10 warning signs I've missed before." Don't overthink it, just let the memories flow. Maybe your list includes things like: "interrupts me when I talk," "downplays my achievements," "gets angry when I say no," "refuses to apologize," or "makes fun of my boundaries." The goal is to get really specific about what has led to trouble in past relationships, whether romantic, professional, or even within your family.

When you finish your list, keep it somewhere handy. This isn't just for reflection; it's a practical tool. Before starting something new, a date, a friendship, or a job interview, review your checklist and remind yourself of which behaviors you refuse to ignore again. For example, if you're beginning a new job and you see your manager badmouthing a team member in front of everyone, pause and check your list. Does this match something you've written down? If yes, trust that feeling. If you're meeting someone new and they push past a boundary right out of the gate, practice saying, "I need you to respect my boundaries," or "I'm not comfortable with that," to reinforce your limits.

Patterns aren't static; they shift as you grow and learn. New experiences might reveal red flags you hadn't even considered. You may notice now that someone who pressures you for immediate closeness tends to expect too much emotional labor from you down the line. Or perhaps you've realized a co-worker who always plays the victim leaves you feeling guilty for things beyond your control. Keep updating your list as these patterns emerge. Ask yourself every few months: "What new red flags have I noticed lately?" Write them down without judgment; this is how you get wiser with each relationship.

One common struggle is self-doubt when a red flag pops up. You might think, "Is this really a warning or just my anxiety?" Clarify how to distinguish genuine red flags from misinterpretations to prevent unnecessary self-doubt. When you notice a warning sign, pause and take a breath. Try saying out loud or writing: "I notice this red flag, what small step can I take to protect myself?" This might mean slowing down a relationship, asking more questions, or simply stepping back for now. Remember, one red flag is enough to pause and reassess; don't wait until you have a handful.

Reframing how you view red flags is powerful. Instead of seeing them as accusations or proof that someone is "bad," view them as information about what does or doesn't work for you. It's not about being harsh; it's about keeping yourself safe and healthy. If your checklist helps you spot an unhealthy pattern early, that's self-care in action. It doesn't matter if someone else would tolerate the behavior; your boundaries are valid because they're yours.

Over time, using your personal red flag checklist becomes second nature. It lets you walk into new situations with more clarity and less fear of repeating old mistakes. You're not looking for perfection in others; you're looking for honest signals that deserve your attention. Each time you trust your checklist, you build self-trust and move closer to the kind of relationships where you can relax, be yourself, and thrive.

How to Vet for Toxic Traits Early When Dating and Building New Friendships

Meeting someone new can be exciting but also nerve-wracking, especially if previous experiences have left you second-guessing your instincts. Approaching new relationships with curiosity and caution helps you feel safer. Asking thoughtful questions, making careful observations, and taking your time can protect you from repeating old, unhealthy patterns.

Please pay close attention to both what people say and what they don't, focusing on open-ended questions that invite genuine reflection. For example, asking, "How do you handle disagreements with friends?" reveals much more than small talk. Look for answers that show communication and compromise, rather than blaming others or avoiding the issue. Be aware of subtle red flags, such as dismissive body language, inconsistent stories, or avoidance of accountability. Questions about their family relationships offer additional insight, not into family details, but into how they handle flaws and responsibility. Someone who always paints themselves as a victim or talks about constant drama may lack self-awareness and empathy, which are key qualities to look for.

Notice if someone's early behavior feels "too good to be true." Tactics like love-bombing, excessive flattery, grand gestures, or premature declarations of deep feelings should signal caution. Another tactic is "fast-forwarding" intimacy by sharing intense personal stories immediately, creating a false sense of closeness and pressure to reciprocate. Pay attention to how someone reacts if you express a need for slow pacing; if they tease, push back, or ignore your boundaries, it's a warning sign. These behaviors may seem flattering at first, but they often mask a need for control or a rapid emotional attachment.

Try adopting a "slow reveal" strategy, taking your time before sharing personal details or making quick commitments. You're under no obligation to share your life story upfront. Set boundaries on how often you communicate and what you share (e.g., limiting texting or meeting only in public until you're comfortable). Observe how your boundaries are received; a respectful response is an encouraging sign for the future.

If you notice red flags like disrespect for your boundaries, gossip, or emotional dismissiveness, it's okay to step back or end contact without guilt or lengthy explanations. Here are some simple ways to step back: "I'm not feeling a connection, but I wish you well," or "I need to focus on other things." You don't have to elaborate. If pressed, repeat yourself once and don't feel pressured to respond further. Your peace and comfort come first.

To help decide how to proceed, use a quick self-check after each interaction: Did I feel heard? Was there mutual respect? Did I feel safe sharing my thoughts? If the answer to any is "no," use that as a sign to pause or reconsider your involvement. Trust your gut responses; relationships should make you feel secure and valued, not anxious or uncertain.

For a practical approach, keep a note on your phone or in a journal with your screening questions and the check-in list. Please review them before future meetups and reflect after each interaction. This habit helps you spot unhealthy patterns faster and strengthens your ability to choose better relationships.

Proactively screening new acquaintances might feel awkward if you're used to giving people the benefit of the doubt, but pacing yourself and setting boundaries isn't rude; it's self-respect. The right people will appreciate your caution and respond with respect. It's natural for excitement or nerves to cloud judgment, but these strategies can help you remain grounded and self-aware.

You won't always catch every warning sign or make perfect decisions, so be kind to yourself if you miss something. Every new interaction is a chance to practice; each time you trust your instincts when something feels off, you build stronger self-trust. Real change comes not from expecting perfection, but from acting quickly when you notice concern and protecting yourself before things get complicated.

Teaching Your Children Healthy Boundaries to Stop the Cycle

Raising children to respect boundaries means doing more than giving advice; you need to show them, through daily actions, how to protect themselves and honor others. Start early. Teaching "Your body belongs to you" lays the groundwork for self-trust and consent, not just safety from strangers or inappropriate touch. Use simple, real-life language and games, like asking, "Is this a yes hug or a no hug?" Make it clear that a child can always say no to physical affection, even with family. If your child refuses a hug from Aunt Linda, support them: "That's alright, we can wave instead." Consistently backing them up teaches that their comfort and decisions matter, and that they control what happens to their bodies.

Modeling boundaries yourself is powerful. Kids learn more from what you do than what you say. If you're tired and a neighbor asks for a favor, say to your child, "Thanks for thinking of me, but I need to rest today." Demonstrating a courteous refusal shows how to assert yourself without guilt or drama, and normalizes boundaries rather than making them seem harsh.

Giving children simple scripts for tricky situations helps them feel prepared. Use role-play to practice together. For example, act out: "What if a friend wants you to play a game you don't like?" Have your child practice saying, "No, thank you, I don't want to play that game." Or, "What would you do if someone asked you to keep a secret from me?" Practice responses like, "I would tell you because we keep each other safe." Make this practice routine. Try turning it into a game, switching roles so your child can experience both asserting themselves and responding to pressure.

Children often go along with uncomfortable things to avoid disappointing others or getting in trouble. That's why your reaction is critical if your child tells you someone crossed a boundary, like a classmate stealing a snack or pressuring them to share secrets. Pause, listen, validate their feelings, and say, "Thank you for telling me," or, "It's brave to speak up." Focus on helping them feel safe and heard before problem-solving or assigning blame.

Keep empowering your child by reminding them they can always come to you if something feels wrong. Be clear: "You can always tell me if someone makes you uncomfortable. I will listen, and you won't get in trouble." Some families set up a "safe word," a silly code the child can use to signal they need help or want to leave an uncomfortable situation. For example, if your child says, "Pineapple pizza," you know it's time to check in or intervene privately.

Teaching emotional boundaries is just as important. Explain that everyone manages their own feelings. If a friend says, "If you don't play with me, I'll be sad forever," coach your child to respond, "I'm sorry you're sad, but I still need some space." Help them avoid taking on guilt for someone else's emotions when they're simply advocating for themselves.

Children flourish when they know their feelings matter and their voice counts. Use stories, books, and TV shows as opportunities: pause when characters navigate boundaries and discuss together. Ask, "How do you think she felt when her friend didn't listen?" or "What could he have done differently?" These discussions teach empathy and relationship skills.

As your children get older, revisit and adjust these lessons for their age. Focus on body autonomy and simple scripts with young kids. With older children, discuss more complex issues like digital boundaries, emotional safety, and peer pressure. Keep communication open and regularly check in about their friends and experiences at school. Normalize boundary talk at home, share your own challenges and successes. When children see adults model self-respect and compassion, they learn not just to protect themselves, but also how to build safer, kinder communities as they grow.

Navigating Social Media and Digital Boundaries

Social media and digital spaces make it easier to connect with others, share our lives, and build new relationships. However, these platforms bring distinct risks that can quickly lead to stressful or toxic situations. The dark side may appear when a toxic ex monitors your stories, likes old photos, or contacts you through mutual friends. Or you're in a group chat where someone incites drama, shares private messages, or gossips. These behaviors, from stalking to public shaming, can erode your peace of mind.

Toxic digital behaviors appear in many ways, including cyberbullying, trolling, persistent messaging, and triangulation. Unlike face-to-face interactions, online abuse is harder to escape and can be relentless. You might receive unwanted messages at all hours, be repeatedly tagged in uncomfortable posts, or feel pressured to respond to others' demands. Even minor actions, such as a casual "like," can be twisted to fuel gossip or manipulation. Online drama can feel inescapable, following you wherever you go through notifications and messages, which may heighten anxiety and isolation.

Managing your digital boundaries begins with controlling who can see and engage with your content. Regularly review privacy settings across platforms like Facebook, Instagram, WhatsApp, TikTok, and LinkedIn. Update these frequently, as settings often change. Limit your posts to trusted contacts, remove unknown followers, and use block or mute features when needed. There's no shame in protecting your mental space. If someone keeps tagging you or sharing posts that make you uncomfortable, clearly ask them to stop ("Please don't tag me without my permission"). If your boundary is ignored, restrict their access using platform tools.

Group chats, whether with friends, family, or colleagues, require specific attention. Toxicity often manifests as constant criticism, endless arguments, or one person dominating while others walk on eggshells. If a group chat causes you more stress than support, it's okay to mute or archive it. You don't need to explain unless you wish to. If you choose to leave, a simple note like "I'm leaving this chat to focus on my well-being" is sufficient. Your peace comes before group expectations.

Work-related digital spaces can also be problematic, think passive-aggressive emails, after-hours messages, or colleagues who use "reply all" to shame others. Keep responses brief and professional. Set clear boundaries for your working hours and availability. For any inappropriate comments or harassment in emails or on work apps such as *Slack* or *Teams*, document the incidents and contact HR if needed.

Digital self-care isn't just about defense; it's about cultivating a healthier online environment. Schedule regular breaks from social media; a weekly "detox" day can help reset your mind and reduce anxiety. Unfollow or mute accounts that drain your energy, trigger unfavorable comparisons, or spark conflict. Prioritize following uplifting pages and communities focused on encouragement and support; mindfully curating your feed is a form of self-respect.

Small habits help build intentional digital boundaries. Set reminders, like "Social media break every Sunday" or "Unfollow three draining accounts this week," to support healthier routines. Limit message checks to certain times of the day. If you notice yourself getting caught in drama or endless scrolling, pause and shift attention to something offline and positive.

Remember, your digital boundaries are just as valid as those you set in person. Blocking someone who makes you feel unsafe or uncomfortable is not rude. You're not obligated to accept every friend request or reply to every message. Muting someone lets you maintain peace without confrontation. In situations where you can't leave a toxic digital space (like at work), minimize your participation and focus on safe, neutral topics.

If a digital space turns toxic, trust your instincts. If something feels off, you have the right to distance yourself, even if others downplay your concerns. Your online well-being comes before anyone's expectations about your availability. Digital boundaries are a continual process, and each minor adjustment helps you enjoy technology on your terms.

When to Seek Professional Help Through Therapy, Support Groups, and Legal Resources

Sometimes, despite your best efforts, things don't get better. You may find yourself going in circles, feeling overwhelmed, or unable to shake the anxiety that keeps you up at night. You may have tried setting boundaries, switching up your approach, or leaning on friends, but nothing has stuck. If you're facing constant distress, or if safety, emotional, or physical concerns have become serious, consider reaching out for outside help. There could be a legal threat hanging over your head, or you could keep ending up in the same confusing situations, no matter what you do. These are all signs that more support could make a real difference.

Take a moment and check in with yourself. Are you feeling persistently anxious, hopeless, or afraid? Has your sleep or appetite changed? Do you find yourself avoiding work, family events, or even simple phone calls out of fear? If there's ever a sense of danger, whether from someone's words, threats, or actions, don't wait. The same goes if you've made repeated attempts to shift the dynamic on your own and it's just not working. Here's a simple list to keep in mind: if you feel unsafe, trapped, hopeless, isolated, or stuck in patterns that won't budge, seeking help is a strong next step.

Finding a therapist or counselor can seem intimidating at first. You might wonder how to pick the right person or what to expect in those first conversations. Start by thinking about what matters most to you: Do you want someone with expertise in unhealthy relationships or trauma? Are you looking for a specific communication style, direct, gentle, or solution-focused? It's okay to "interview" therapists before settling on one. Ask direct questions: "What experience do you have with toxic relationships?" or "How do you handle confidentiality?" Notice how you feel with them, do you feel heard and respected? Green flags include empathy, non-judgment, and clarity about the process. Red flags are therapists who dismiss your feelings, rush you, or seem distracted. You should never feel pressured to stay with someone who doesn't feel like a good fit. Useful directories such as Psychology Today, TherapyDen, or local mental health hotlines can help you get started.

Support groups, whether online or in person, offer another powerful resource. These can be led by peers who've been through similar experiences or by trained professionals. Peer-led groups tend to focus on shared stories and mutual validation. Professional-led groups may offer structured tools, education, and support. Think about what you need most right now: Is it advice and practical tips? Or do you crave connection and the relief that comes from knowing others truly get it? Look for groups that set ground rules about confidentiality and respect. It's normal to try a few before finding one that fits.

When situations escalate to threats, stalking, harassment, or custody battles, knowing your legal rights matters. Protection orders (sometimes called restraining orders) can create space and safety when someone won't respect boundaries. If workplace harassment is involved, agencies like the Equal Employment Opportunity Commission (EEOC) can help you understand your options. For child custody issues tied to toxicity or abuse, family law professionals or legal aid societies are vital. If money is tight, many communities offer free or reduced-cost legal clinics, search for local domestic violence hotlines or legal aid directories for help. When preparing for a consult, bring documentation: dates and times of incidents, copies of threatening messages or emails, notes on conversations, and any witnesses, if possible.

It's important to remember that asking for help isn't a failure; it's a sign of courage and self-respect. No one expects you to carry everything on your own. There are times when outside expertise is what turns the tide and brings real change within reach. If you've hesitated out of fear of judgment or stigma, repeat this affirmation: "Seeking help is an empowered choice." You're not weak for needing support; in fact, recognizing when to ask for it is one of the strongest things you can do for yourself.

As you move forward, whether things feel chaotic or just a bit off, professional help is always an option in your toolkit. It doesn't mean giving up control; it means adding new allies and resources as you build a safer life.

You have practical tools for spotting problems early and breaking old cycles, but sometimes outside support is the missing piece. Trusting yourself enough to ask for help when needed is part of growing stronger, not just surviving, but moving toward something better. Next up: Let's talk about thriving beyond survival, what it looks like to live fully after toxic relationships fade into the background.

Chapter Ten

Live Free and Thrive Beyond Toxic Relationships

Designing a Life That Attracts Healthy Relationships

Once again, you're standing in the kitchen, sunlight pouring in, coffee in hand, not with chest-tightening tension or dread about unpredictable messages. Instead, you feel steady and secure, trusting your instincts and knowing the people in your life truly respect you. This ease isn't luck, but the outcome of conscious choices: who you invite close and how you show up for yourself. If you've lived in survival mode, enduring toxic partners, friends, or relatives, peace might seem unfamiliar. But a life with healthy, mutual relationships isn't out of reach; it starts with understanding your values, clarifying what matters to you, and intentionally shaping your social circle. You never have to settle for less.

The process begins with asking: What do I want in my relationships? Those who grew up in environments of inconsistency or manipulation often haven't asked themselves this vital question. Instead of falling into relationships out of old habit or loneliness, pause to define your desires, values, and non-negotiables. Do you value reliability, laughter, and meaningful conversation? Do you want vulnerability met with kindness or respectful conflict resolution? These standards set your compass. Respect and compassion aren't optional; reciprocity is a must. Ignore anyone who resists mutual care or disrespects your boundaries.

Ask, "What Do I Want to Experience in My Relationships?"

Take a moment to clarify your relationship essentials in a notebook or notes app.

- **List three feelings you desire with others:** e.g., safe, accepted, energized.

- **Write your top five relationship values:** e.g., honesty, kindness, humor, loyalty, open-mindedness.

- **Name three deal-breaker behaviors:** e.g., disrespect, manipulation, and jealousy.

- **Describe your ideal interaction:** e.g., "Balanced conversation, I listen and am listened to."

- **Recall moments you felt seen or valued:** What made those experiences unique?

This list isn't a wish, it's your baseline. When you're clear on your priorities, you spot both warning signs and healthy signals early. Healthy relationships don't require perfection; they need consistent patterns of feeling safe and respected.

Once your compass is set, consider where and how to meet people who share your values. After toxic experiences, it's natural to retreat, but isolation doesn't promote healing. Rather than waiting for good people to appear, intentionally seek out environments where your interests and values are reflected. Attend book clubs, art classes, hiking groups, gym classes, or yoga meetups, whatever matches your priorities. Volunteering connects you with those who value giving back. Even professional networks can foster connections rooted in authenticity.

If joining a new group feels intimidating, bring a friend or let the organizer know you're new for added support. The goal isn't to stay busy but to engage with people who value what you do. When you're yourself, not over-accommodating or shrinking away, you naturally attract authenticity.

Recognizing green flags can make you feel hopeful and reassured that healthy relationships are possible. Notice behaviors like trustworthiness and genuine interest to build confidence in your ability to connect authentically.

Consistency is key: notice if their kindness is steady or unpredictable. Empathy might show up as someone noticing your mood and checking in, or celebrating your wins rather than competing. Sincere apologies, rather than defensive ones, are invaluable.

When you see these green flags, take small steps to build the relationship. Say, "I enjoyed our talk, want to grab a coffee?" Small invitations establish trust and slowly deepen connection.

Be intentional about how you present yourself, not by performing, but by showing healthy openness and boundaries. People pick up on whether you're approachable and sincere, or distant. Practice sharing small pieces of yourself: a story, a recent struggle, or even the fact that you're nervous about joining a new group.

Vulnerability here isn't about sharing everything, but signaling how you value more than superficial small talk. You can say, "I appreciate honesty and try to offer it too." This communicates your priorities clearly.

Healthy people are drawn to authenticity and will respect boundaries presented kindly. Statements like "I'm working on being more open about my feelings" or "I need downtime sometimes" show self-awareness and self-respect, attracting people who value directness rather than drama.

If old fears surface, the anxiety that being yourself will push others away, remind yourself that genuine relationships rely on honesty and mutual care, not endless self-sacrifice or hiding. Remember, setbacks are normal; each small step builds confidence over time.

Taking small steps in building connections can help you feel patient and encouraged. Responding to respectful messages or initiating with a simple gesture nurtures trust and confidence over time.

As new connections form, regularly check in with yourself: Am I respected? Do I feel energized after time together? Are there subtle red flags, such as dismissiveness or inconsistency? If discomfort or subtle red flags arise, trust yourself to set boundaries or step back.

Signs of Healthy Relationships

- Conversation is balanced with mutual listening and sharing.
- Disagreements are handled respectfully; no shaming or silent treatments.
- Sincere apologies are never deflective; they never deflect blame.
- Boundaries are respected without conflict.
- Growth and achievements are celebrated, not competed with.
- Humor remains kind and light.
- Support is shown through actions, not just words.
- All emotions, even difficult ones, are met with empathy, not dismissal.

Check most boxes most of the time? That's worth investing in. If not, trust your gut even if things appear fine.

Practice communicating your values early, not as ultimatums, but invitations for honesty. Try scripts like, "I value direct communication," or "I'm looking for mutual support in friendships."

Healthy relationships are built on consistent small acts of trust, not grand gestures. If someone shows up, listens, and meets you with kindness, even imperfectly, they're revealing their true character.

You now have the power to curate your life, choosing who belongs and what's acceptable with clarity. The more intentionally you build spaces and relationships aligning with your values, the more peaceful and sunny those coffee moments become as your new normal.

Daily Boundary Rituals that Create Habits for Long-Term Emotional Safety

Routines can anchor you and protect your peace, especially after chaotic times. Boundaries aren't just rules set once; they're daily habits woven into your life. Starting each morning with a simple affirmation, like "I am allowed to protect my energy today," can shift your mindset for the day. These affirmations are constant reminders that you control what you allow in. If you're used to putting others first or feel guilty saying no, this will feel awkward at first, but it grows easier with practice. On tougher days, repeat the affirmation as needed. This practice is about progress, not perfection. To reinforce it, keep reminders visible, on a mirror or as a phone alarm, so you continually realign with your intentions.

Boundary rituals continue throughout the day. Regular self-check-ins help you catch boundary slips early. Imagine a mental traffic light: green means safe and respected, yellow signals caution or discomfort, and red means a limit has been or is about to be crossed. Ask, "What color am I right now?" This makes your emotional state concrete and actionable. If you're green, savor the safety; in yellow, slow down and breathe. For example, when someone bombards you with requests or texts, pause to decide if you need a firmer response before you hit red. If you're in the red zone, feeling anxious, angry, or needing to escape, that's your cue to enforce a boundary immediately, whether by stepping out or directly saying, "I need to stop this conversation." Remaining aware in this way is like having a radar for your emotional safety.

Evenings are a time for reflection. Use a notebook or your phone to check in by asking, "Where did I honor my boundaries today? Where did I struggle?" Don't judge, note your progress. If you refused a task or ignored a guilt-tripping text, that's growth. If you gave in or let resentment build, write it with self-compassion. Regular reflection, written, recorded, or mental, helps you notice which situations or people most test your boundaries, making it easier to plan.

Planning for high-risk situations adds another layer of self-care. If you know that certain people or events stress your boundaries (a critical parent, a demanding boss), prepare in advance. Have simple scripts ready, like "Let me get back to you tomorrow," so you're not pressured into immediate answers. Save scripts in your phone for quick replies. Visual cues, such as a sticky note on your laptop that says "Pause before responding," can help interrupt autopilot people-pleasing.

It's tough to maintain new habits alone, especially under stress or in the face of confrontation. That's why having an accountability partner, a friend, sibling, therapist, or online peer who's also working on boundaries, can be powerful. Check in weekly about your wins and challenges, whether by call, text, emoji, or voice note. Sharing makes progress real and helps break isolation. If no one close fits this role, look for supportive boundary-setting groups, in person or online. Reading or hearing others' stories reminds you that setbacks are normal and that growth is gradual.

For more structure, try a weekly review each Sunday night. Make it a ritual: light a candle or play music. List three times you held a boundary and reflect on how you felt. Then, note one area you struggled in and make a plan for next time (e.g., "If Mom brings up politics, I'll change the subject or excuse myself"). Over time, this ritual builds self-trust and tracks your progress.

PRACTICAL WAYS TO PROTECT YOURSELF FROM TOXIC PEOPLE

If you're a visual thinker, draw boundary circles: put yourself in the center, add rings for work, family, friends, and other areas, and use color codes, green for healthy, yellow for caution, and red for areas where limits must be strengthened. This gives you a quick overview of where to direct your energy.

During especially stressful days, family holidays, or urgent work deadlines, keep pre-written reminders handy on your phone: "I am not responsible for fixing others' feelings," "It's okay to leave if things get heated," or "My needs are valid." Reading these before challenging moments keeps you grounded and helps prevent old habits from taking over.

Before engaging with people who challenge your boundaries, rehearse boundary statements aloud so they're easier to say when it counts: "I'm not discussing that," "I need space," or "No, thank you." Practicing with a mirror or partner makes these words more natural under pressure.

It's easy to internalize the idea that boundaries are selfish or cold if you've been told so by toxic people. But steady rituals teach your mind and body that protecting yourself is both allowed and essential for emotional health.

You can pair boundary rituals with enjoyable self-care activities: try journaling while having tea, stretch and recall boundary wins, or set intentions before social events during your walk.

For digital overwhelm, schedule mini digital detoxes as part of your routine. Turn off notifications during meals or designate screen-free times.

Remember, rituals should feel supportive, not like rigid rules or chores. Adjust them as needed so they help you, not overwhelm you.

Healthy boundaries aren't about never being triggered, but about recovering quickly from slips and learning, instead of wallowing in shame.

Daily boundary rituals, morning affirmations, midday check-ins, preset texts for sticky moments, and honest chats with supportive people add up over time. They help create an environment where healthy relationships flourish by starting with self-care and self-respect.

As long as these habits fit messy, real life, they'll reinforce that healthy boundaries aren't just possible, they're your right, every day.

Celebrating Progress to Honor Your Journey and Stay Empowered

Progress doesn't always announce itself with fanfare or fireworks. Sometimes, it's found in the pause before you say yes to a favor you don't want to do. Other times, it's the moment you realize you're not treading on eggshells during a phone call with a family member. You might spot it in the steady beat of your own heart after declining a guilt trip or in the quiet confidence that follows a respectful "no." Too often, growth hides in these small acts, easily missed if you're only looking for dramatic breakthroughs. When you've spent years in unhealthy dynamics, it's easy to overlook how far you've come. That's why intentionally marking your progress matters. It isn't just about feeling good, it's about wiring your brain for resilience and self-worth, giving yourself evidence that change is real, and making sure you never forget it.

You can make celebrating your own growth a habit. One creative practice is to keep a "milestone jar." Every time you notice yourself doing something new, speaking up, saying no, walking away from chaos, or even taking time for yourself, write it down on a slip of paper. Toss it into the jar. On hard days, pull one out and read it back as proof that setbacks don't erase progress. It doesn't have to be fancy; a mason jar, a shoebox, or even a notes app works. The point is, your victories are worth capturing and revisiting.

Some milestones feel bigger and deserve their own ritual. You could finally end contact with someone who never respected your boundaries. Perhaps you left a toxic job or went a whole month without letting someone else's drama control your mood. These moments can be marked with simple ceremonies, acts that turn invisible wins into visible memories. Light a candle and sit quietly, letting the soft glow remind you of how far you've come. Or plant a flower or small tree, watching it grow as a living symbol of your decision to choose yourself over chaos. These actions send strong signals to your mind: this matters, I matter, and my growth is real.

There's also power in writing letters to yourself. Take some time to write to the version of you who was once stuck, maybe last year or five years ago, who didn't know how to say no or thought peace wasn't possible. Tell that past self what you're proud of. List out every time you stood up for yourself or walked away from something that hurt. Be gentle and specific: "You didn't know better then, but you learned." This isn't about shaming who you were; it's about honoring all the steps that brought you here. Reread these letters when doubts creep in or when progress feels slow.

Sometimes sharing your story with others deepens your sense of meaning and anchors your growth even further. You don't have to post every detail on social media or become a motivational speaker. Even a small act of leaving an anonymous message on a forum, offering encouragement in a support group, or talking honestly with a trusted friend, can turn pain into purpose. Sharing isn't just for others; it helps you see yourself as capable and wise, not just wounded. When someone else says, "That helped me," you realize your struggles have value beyond survival.

If you want to try this out, use a simple script: "What I wish I'd known about boundaries..." and fill in the rest with your own truth. Maybe it's that boundaries aren't mean, or that saying no doesn't make you unlovable, or that healing is slow but worth every awkward step. You could post this as an update in an online group or offer to moderate a discussion for newcomers. Helping others breaks the spell of isolation that toxic relationships often create.

Celebrating progress also means getting creative with rewards that reinforce new habits. Treat yourself to something small, a favorite meal, an afternoon off, a new book, whenever you hit a milestone that once felt impossible. These rewards aren't bribes; they're reminders that you're building a life where self-care is honored, not just squeezed in around other people's demands.

Of course, not every day feels like winning. Real growth happens in fits and starts, good days followed by setbacks or frustration. Maybe you snapped at someone when you wanted to be calm, or gave in when you meant to hold firm. It's tempting to beat yourself up or think all progress is lost. This is where self-compassion becomes a lifeline. Remind yourself that healing isn't linear. There will be zigzags and loops backward along the way, but every step forward counts, even if it's tiny or quickly followed by two steps back.

On days when motivation dips and setbacks sting, lean on simple affirmations: "Progress isn't always straight; every step counts." Repeat this until it feels true again. If negative self-talk gets loud ("I'm back where I started," or "I'll never get this right"), counter with kinder responses: "It's okay to rest and regroup," "Getting stuck doesn't erase what I've already learned," "Tomorrow is another chance." Write these down somewhere visible, a sticky note on your fridge, an alert on your phone, or say them out loud in the shower.

Another helpful strategy is keeping a "setback survival kit." This can be as simple as a list of things that help you bounce back: listening to music that lifts your mood, taking a walk outside, texting a supportive friend, reading an encouraging message from your milestone jar, or revisiting your letter to yourself. The key is remembering that setbacks are part of the process, not proof of failure, but evidence that growth takes real effort over time.

Reflecting on your journey can also mean looking for patterns in what helps you keep going. You may notice that after sharing a win with someone who understands, motivation soars for days. Or seeing concrete reminders, a plant from your ceremony or slips from your milestone jar, keeps hope alive when everything feels slow. Gathering these insights isn't about rigidly sticking to rituals but about noticing what truly fuels your resilience.

Don't be afraid to shake things up if old ways lose their spark. If lighting candles no longer feels meaningful, try painting a progress stone for every victory and lining them on your windowsill. If writing letters feels stale, record voice messages to your future self. Adapt celebration practices so they stay fresh and personal rather than becoming another chore.

Also consider reconnecting with others who are walking similar paths, not just for support during challenging times, but also to recognize growth together. There may be someone in your life who has also learned hard lessons about boundaries and respect; celebrate both of your wins over coffee or through shared texts. Mutual encouragement doubles the power of personal progress.

The more often you recognize and mark your victories, no matter how small, the more likely you are to keep moving forward even when things get messy or complicated. This ongoing celebration rewires your mind away from old scripts of shame and failure toward new beliefs in your own strength.

Ultimately, honoring your progress isn't about perfection or constant forward motion; it's about making space for every part of the process: every effort, setback, rest, and renewal. When you build regular habits of celebration into daily life, through jars, letters, ceremonies, and tiny rewards, you turn invisible growth into something tangible and memorable.

As this chapter draws to a close, remember: every act of self-care and every step toward healthier relationships deserves recognition. Growth looks like many things, sometimes bold leaps forward, occasionally small shifts only you notice at first, but none of it is wasted. You've learned how to protect yourself from toxicity and build bridges to better connections; now let celebration fuel even greater change ahead.

Conclusion

Take a breath and look at where you are now. Seriously, pause for a second. You've made it to the end of a book that, let's be honest, covers some tough ground. If you're feeling a little lighter, more precise, or even just more validated than when you started, that's no accident. You've traveled from the fog of confusion and self-doubt that toxic people create straight into a place of clarity, solid self-trust, and a toolkit of real-life skills. That's not a small thing; it's a huge accomplishment. I hope you feel proud, because you have every right to.

This journey wasn't just about learning what toxic behavior looks like from a safe distance. You dug into the gritty details, how manipulation works, why it happens, and how it can sneak into even the most "normal" relationships. You took the time to map out your own triggers and patterns, and you discovered that you are not stuck with the roles or habits handed to you. You learned that your boundaries matter, and that setting them isn't selfish, it's self-care, even when it feels awkward at first.

We covered a lot of ground together. You learned how to spot toxic patterns and early red flags, so you can trust your gut rather than second-guess yourself. You got scripts and strategies for everything from shutting down workplace drama to handling family guilt trips and "jokes" that don't feel funny. You practiced ways to keep your cool in challenging conversations and learned to hold your own, even with people who push back hard. You saw that healing from emotional wounds, especially after gaslighting or long-term manipulation, is possible, even if it's not always quick or easy.

PRACTICAL WAYS TO PROTECT YOURSELF FROM TOXIC PEOPLE

You might not realize it right now, but you now have a set of tools that can change your life. You know the difference between healthy conflict and toxic cycles. You can name and respond to classic manipulation tactics. You have words to protect your peace, and checklists to help you spot when things are going sideways. You've got self-care routines for the days when setting boundaries feels impossible, and you know it's okay to need time to recover and regroup.

If you're still in a relationship or situation where you can't "just walk away," I see you. I want you to know that this doesn't make you weak or broken. Sometimes staying is necessary for a while, and sometimes leaving just isn't possible yet. Progress isn't always a clean break or a dramatic exit. Sometimes it's the quiet, stubborn act of saying, "No, not today," or "That's enough for now." Every step counts. Every time you pause before reacting, every time you journal your feelings instead of swallowing them, every time you stand up for yourself, you're moving forward.

Healing from toxic relationships is not a straight line. Some days you'll feel strong, and other days you might slip into old patterns or doubt your progress. When that happens, remind yourself that setbacks are normal. Be gentle with yourself, offer compassion, and remember that each new attempt is part of your growth. Rest, seek support, and try again tomorrow-your resilience is building with every step.

I want to encourage you to use what you've learned here. Pull out those scripts when you need them. Revisit your red flag checklist before a new friendship or date. Practice your boundary-setting phrases in the mirror (it really helps). Keep your self-care routines in your calendar, not just as a backup plan but as a non-negotiable part of your week. When things get tough, reach out, talk to a trusted friend, a support group, or a professional who "gets it." You don't have to do this alone.

And don't forget to celebrate your progress. Seriously! Mark your milestones. Journal about the moments you spoke up, even if your voice shook. Sharing your story can inspire hope in others. Every small step, every act of self-care, is a sign of your growing strength and resilience.

This journey doesn't end with the last page of a book. You're not just surviving anymore, you're learning how to thrive. Keep refining your checklists. Practice those new habits until they become natural. Notice when relationships feel safe and easy, and invest more of your energy there. Healthy connection is a skill, and you're building it, one day at a time.

If you ever feel stuck or overwhelmed, remember that you have a whole section of resources to lean on, glossaries, checklists, and suggestions for professional help. Keep these tools handy. Knowing where to turn can provide reassurance and ongoing support, helping you feel more confident in your healing journey.

Above all, know this: your worthiness and right to healthy love are absolute. No matter how long you've been caught in toxic cycles, you are not doomed to repeat them. You are not too damaged or too late to start over. Every choice you make to protect your peace and honor your needs affirms your value, even if it feels small.

Thank you for trusting me to be part of your journey. I wrote this book because I believe in your ability to change your story, at your own pace, in your own way. I hope you'll carry these tools with you and keep choosing yourself every single day. The path ahead is yours to shape, and I can't wait for you to see just how strong, worthy, and free you truly are.

More people may also benefit from the information in this book. However, they need your help. If you found this book worthwhile and informative, please leave an honest review to help others recognize the value of this resource. Thank you. — George Munson

PRACTICAL WAYS TO PROTECT YOURSELF FROM TOXIC PEOPLE

References

10 Signs of a Toxic Boss — and How to Protect Yourself. (2025, February 6). Harvard Business Review. https://hbr.org/2025/02/10-signs-of-a-toxic-boss-and-how-to-protect-yourself

Admin. (2017, February 13). *Your guide to documenting proof of a hostile work environment.* https://www.skillsusa-wi.org/wordpress/your-guide-to-documenting-proof-of-a-hostile-work-environment/#:~:text=Record%20Each%20Incident%3A%20Each%20time,language%2C%20gestures%2C%20or%20actions.

Alliance. (2023, August 16). *8 Ways to Teach Kids about Consent and Healthy Boundaries.* Connecticut Alliance to End Sexual Violence. https://endsexualviolencect.org/8-ways-to-teach-kids-about-consent-and-healthy-boundaries/

Be Ceremonial. (2024, April 28). *Boundaries rituals - be ceremonial.* https://www.beceremonial.com/daily-rituals/needs/boundaries/

Bernstein, J., PhD. (2022, December 25). Staying emotionally healthy when your parents are hurtful. *Psychology Today.* https://www.psychologytoday.com/us/blog/liking-the-child-you-love/202212/setting-boundaries-with-your-gaslighting-parents

Biali, S., MD. (2013, April 30). Setting a healthy boundary will make people mad - but don't let that stop you. *Psychology Today.*

https://www.psychologytoday.com/us/blog/prescriptions-life/201304/if-you-set-boundary-expect-deal-anger

Center, B. a. C. (2025, August 4). Top 10 manipulation tactics and how to Counter them | Bay Area CBT Center. *Bay Area CBT Center.* https://bayareacbtcenter.com/top-10-manipulation-tactics-and-how-to-counter-them/

Clinic, C. (2025, July 14). *What is gaslighting? Here's what to do if you think it's happening to you.* Cleveland Clinic. https://health.clevelandclinic.org/gaslighting

Detaching with Love: Setting boundaries with difficult elderly parents. (n.d.). © 2007-2025 AgingCare All Rights Reserved. https://www.agingcare.com/articles/setting-boundaries-with-parents-who-are-abusive-142804.htm

England, A. (2025, October 30). *What the term 'Flying monkeys' means when we talk about narcissism.* Verywell Mind. https://www.verywellmind.com/narcissists-and-flying-monkeys-7552473

Equalitync. (2025, June 24). *How to Build a Chosen Family: practical tips and community stories | Equality North Carolina.* Equality North Carolina. https://equalitync.org/2025/02/21/blog-how-to-build-a-chosen-family-practical-tips-and-community-stories/

Forth, A., Sezlik, S., Lee, S., Ritchie, M., Logan, J., & Ellingwood, H. (2021). Toxic Relationships: The experiences and effects of psychopathy in romantic relationships. *International Journal of Offender Therapy and Comparative Criminology, 66*(15), 1627–1658. https://doi.org/10.1177/0306624x211049187

Gonzalez, A. (2025, January 15). *Healthy vs. Unhealthy Relationships.* WebMD. https://www.webmd.com/sex-relationships/healthy-vs-unhealthy-relationships

Gupta, S. (2025, September 19). *How to recognize emotional blackmail and protect yourself*. Verywell Mind. https://www.verywellmind.com/emotional-blackmail-7974647

Harassment. (n.d.). U.S. Equal Employment Opportunity Commission. https://www.eeoc.gov/harassment

Heallth, P. B. (2024, December 9). *How toxic relationships affect your mental health | Prime Behavioral Health*. Prime Behavioral Health. https://primebehavioralhealth.com/blog/how-toxic-relationships-affect-your-mental-health/

How to identify and manage your emotional triggers. (2020, November 13). Healthline. https://www.healthline.com/health/mental-health/emotional-triggers

How to set boundaries and why it matters for your mental health | Cultivating Health. (2025, August 23). *cultivating-health*. https://health.ucdavis.edu/blog/cultivating-health/how-to-set-boundaries-and-why-it-matters-for-your-mental-health/2024/03

Huizen, J. (2024, March 22). *Examples and signs of gaslighting and how to respond*. https://www.medicalnewstoday.com/articles/gaslighting

Jacobs, S. (2024, April 9). *Parallel Parenting: A Solution for Co-Parenting with a Narcissist*. TalkingParents. https://talkingparents.com/blog/parallel-parenting-with-narcissist

Jaime, & Jaime. (2025, April 14). How to Set Boundaries with a Toxic Family (Without the Guilt) -. *The Princess & The Prosthetic - Embracing Our Perfectly Imperfect Fairy Tale*. https://theprincessandtheprostheticblog.com/2025/05/24/how-to-set-boundaries-with-a-toxic-family-without-the-guilt/

Lc. (2025, November 1). *Understanding Love Bombing vs Genuine Interest After Narcissistic Abuse*. Sallt Sisters. https://salltsisters.com/love-bombing-vs-genuine-interest/

Lpc, J. C. M. (2023, November 28). It may feel stiff or uncaring, but it's highly effective. *Psychology Today*. https://www.psychologytoday.com/us/blog/stress-fracture/202311/how-to-use-scripts-when-communicating-with-a-manipulator

Madeson, M., PhD. (2025, October 9). *Self-Esteem journals, prompts, PDFs, and ideas*. PositivePsychology.com. https://positivepsychology.com/self-esteem-journal-prompts/

MSEd, K. C. (2025, September 26). *How to Stop People-Pleasing*. Verywell Mind. https://www.verywellmind.com/how-to-stop-being-a-people-pleaser-5184412

Navigating Healthy Relationships After toxicity: How Couples therapy Can help. (2025, September 4). *Luxx Therapy in North Richland Hills, TX*. https://www.luxxtherapy.com/blogs/navigating-healthy-relationships-after-toxicity-how-couples-therapy-can-help-2#:~:text=Setting%20healthy%20boundaries%20is%20crucial,look%20back%20on%20if%20needed.

Paul. (2023, March 2). Personal Boundaries: The Only Factor that Makes Social Media "Toxic". *Dr. Paul*. https://drpauldobransky.substack.com/p/boundaries-the-only-thing-thats-wrong

Pham, W. (2025, July 25). Hidden Effects of Gaslighting: A survivor's guide to healing. *Gaslighting Check*. https://www.gaslightingcheck.com/blog/the-hidden-effects-of-gaslighting-a-survivor-s-guide-to-healing-and-recovery

Poitevien, K. W. (2024, July 30). *The "Green flags" of a friendship or relationship*. Philadelphia Counseling for Children and Teens. https://ameltherapy.com/blog/2021/10/5/the-green-flags-of-a-friendship-or-relationship

Raypole, C. (2025, February 20). *30 Grounding techniques to quiet distressing thoughts*. Healthline. https://www.healthline.com/health/grounding-techniques

Villines, Z. (2025, April 10). *What is gray rocking?* https://www.medicalnewstoday.com/articles/grey-rock

WebMD Editorial Contributor. (2024, September 17). *Toxic People: Signs to look for*. WebMD. https://www.webmd.com/mental-health/signs-toxic-person

Young, K. (2020, October 15). Teaching Kids How To Set & Protect Their Boundaries Against Toxic Behaviour - Hey Sigmund. *Hey Sigmund*. https://www.heysigmund.com/teaching-kids-how-to-set-boundaries-and-keep-toxic-people-out/

www.ingramcontent.com/pod-product-compliance
Lightning Source LLC
Chambersburg PA
CBHW070633030426
42337CB00020B/4002